CRYPTO INVESTING FOR BEGINNERS

THE SIMPLE CRYPTOCURRENCY GUIDE TO INVEST IN BITCOIN, ETHEREUM, AND ALTCOINS TO CREATE FINANCIAL FREEDOM

ADAM CHAMBERS

FUNDING FREEDOMS

BRADEM PRESS

This publication is meant as a source of valuable information for the reader, however it is not meant as a substitute for direct expert assistance. If such a level of assistance is required, the services of a competent professional should be sought.

ISBN 978-0-473-61696-0
Bradem Press
New Zealand
2022

Claim your special bonus offer:

Scan Below for free unlimited access to this and all our new books by joining Funding Freedoms Insiders.

SCAN ME

CONTENTS

INTRODUCTION

Four of the five biggest companies in the world are technology companies. Apple tops the list at an impressive 2.1 trillion dollars, followed by Microsoft with 1.8 trillion dollars, and Amazon at 1.6 trillion dollars. It's easy to see why these companies are so valuable—Apple changed phones forever, Microsoft changed computers, and Amazon transformed commerce. What if you had invested in Apple before it made the iPhone? Or in Microsoft before the internet? Or Amazon back when all it sold was books? I am guessing you didn't. Hindsight is 20/20, right? But a new wave is coming. There is a technology that everyone is talking about that has the potential to change the world. That technology is the blockchain, cryptocurrencies, and crypto-assets built upon it. You've likely heard about cryptocurrency or, at least, the more popular Bitcoin. Everywhere you turn, there are stories about someone who has made millions from investing in cryptocurrency. Countless online ads, influencers, and articles urge you to invest.

But what are blockchain, bitcoin, and cryptocurrency? The subject can quickly get over-complicated by experts, and scams abound.

Who can you trust? There are passionate people both supporting bitcoin to the moon and those warning that all crypto is a scam.

So, where can you begin? Here. With this book. Here, we will look at cryptocurrency investing without the fluff, hype, and complexities. Even if you know nothing about crypto and don't know the difference between blockchain and Binance, this book offers a concise and straightforward introduction to the subject. We have written this book because we understand why people are skeptical of this new and fast-evolving field. A few years ago, we were in the same place, knowing crypto was important but with no idea where to begin. Since then, we have learned a lot, and crypto has made a huge impact on our lives. But, while we believe blockchain and cryptocurrency technology will be massively transformative and could be a once-in-a-generation investment opportunity, this is not a crypto sales book. We won't tell you specifically which coin or token to buy. Instead, we will teach you how to research options and choose yourself. This is a book about getting a basic understanding, knowing the risks, and how to protect yourself if you are to wade into this new wild west of finance, technology, and investing.

You will learn three significant things in this book. The first is a broad understanding of bitcoin and cryptocurrencies and how to invest in them. The second is the technology behind cryptocurrencies and, lastly, the practical steps to take to invest.

We will begin by looking at the opportunities presented by cryptocurrencies as an investment option. We look at timing; is it still worth investing in cryptocurrency, or is it too late? After we answer these questions, we will discuss the basis of cryptocurrency and why there is so much hype around it. What are the types and categories? Who controls it? Is Bitcoin money? We will also present the history of Bitcoin, so you have the background you need. We will look at the challenges of investing in cryptocurrency and how to plan your strategy. We will discuss the Why, How, and When:

- Reasons to invest.
- How to Invest.
- How to choose a Currency.
- How to Choose Brokers.
- A step-by-step guide on how you can buy crypto on the world's biggest crypto exchange platform.

We will then discuss when to buy and when to sell. We will explore the principles of long and short-term crypto investing and the features of each option, the benefits attached to both, and how you can decide the best option for you. Our discussion on cryptocurrencies will end with a section on the *12 Things You Need to Know Before You Go Into Cryptocurrency*.

For starters, we will learn about blockchain, which is the technology that makes bitcoin and other cryptocurrencies possible. While blockchain technology may be technically complex, we believe everyone can grasp the basics. We will discuss Crypto-mining (the process through which coins are created). And we will compare crypto to Forex and the more traditional Stock market.

Cryptocurrency is a volatile investment, and it is only right that we discuss the risks involved in cryptocurrency investing. What if bitcoin crashes? Will it ever crash? We will look at the dangers posed by scams and outline how to identify and protect yourself against the most common forms of cryptocurrency scams. Finally, we will weigh these risks against the potential rewards of investing in cryptocurrency. We will also answer the question: if cryptocurrency is volatile, is it worth the risk of investing? We will look at other related issues, such as crypto taxes and how to deal with them, and provide pointers on what to do when the going gets tough, and the market seems red.

By the end of this book, you will have a good understanding of cryptocurrencies and how to begin your investment journey. Before making your first cryptocurrency investment, you will know what questions to ask on your investment journey. We are confident in this book because we have been where you are, with no one to answer the many questions we had about cryptocurrencies. So, with that in mind, we have provided answers to as many questions as possible, big and small. And in that spirit, we will end this book with a Jargon Buster, a list of common jargons used in the crypto world, and provide succinct explanations for them. We understand how difficult it is to hear about crypto and not understand a lot of the terms and concepts. With the Jargon Buster, you'll quickly learn how to speak crypto.

Now that you know what to expect in this book—let's get started!

PART I

THE CRYPTO WORLD

1

THE CRYPTO RUSH

Do You Feel Like You Missed the Boat on Crypto?

"If you invested $100 in bitcoin in 2010, it would have been worth almost $73 million in 2017." Have you come across this statement before? We have. In the past few years, this statement, or some other version of it, has made the rounds all over the internet.

But how could investing $100 have made someone a millionaire so quickly? As unbelievable as it may sound, it's true. In May 2010, Bitcoin was trading at $0.003 per coin. Fast forward to 2021, and Bitcoin reached an all-time high (ATH) of $67,000. Laszlo Hanyecz, an early Bitcoin adopter, spent 10,000 Bitcoins at Papa John's in 2010 to buy two pizzas for himself. The value of his Bitcoins at the time was just $40. For the price of an iPhone, new shoes, or even a cup of coffee, you could have made an investment that would potentially have made you a multi-millionaire today.

Some people took a chance on cryptocurrency a few years ago and are millionaires today. You may know someone personally or have read about some of them. For instance, Erik Finman is regarded as one of the world's youngest bitcoin millionaires. Finman first started investing in cryptocurrencies in 2011, when the price of a bitcoin was around $12. Scott advised buying Bitcoin after he received $1,000 as a gift from his grandma. He made $100,000 by selling his Bitcoin holdings at the end of 2013, when the price was about $1,200 per BTC. In early 2014, he founded Botangle, an education technology startup, with those earnings. Finman got an offer to sell his company in 2015. The investor offered a choice of $100,000 or 300 BTC. The value of a BTC at the time was roughly $200. Finman, on the other hand, was optimistic about the future of bitcoin and chose the 300 BTC option. Finman had 403 bitcoins by the summer of 2017. This investment is valued at roughly $20 million as of 2021.

The logic behind it is simple—early investors and believers, like with any new technology or idea, often receive the most significant rewards because they bear the greatest risk. In this way, cryptocurrency investing has been highly profitable for long-term bitcoin investors and owners willing to take risks. Each time you read about the new Bitcoin prices or watch a video online about someone who changed their lives through investing in crypto, it's easy to criticize yourself for missing the opportunity. But we believe in looking forward and focussing on what you can control. We are still early in the crypto story, and tremendous opportunities remain. Of course, the best time to invest in Bitcoin was several years ago, but if you are willing to take a risk, there may be significant gains in the future. And while you may have failed to do so in the past, all hope is not lost.

We Are Still Early

As the old Chinese proverb says, the best time to plant a tree was twenty years ago, and the next time is now. What you can do right now is grasp the opportunity of the present. You don't have to miss out. As business icon and Virgin founder Richard Branson puts it:

business opportunities are like buses, there's always another one coming.

But is it right for you? It's essential to understand what you invest in. Can you tolerate the risk and volatility? Do you understand the concepts of blockchain and crypto technology? If you're not sure, then don't worry. In this book, we'll cover all these things and more.

Bitcoin and crypto are still in their infancy. Bitcoin was created as recently as 2008, making it less than fifteen years old. In contrast, the internet as we know it was created in the 90s. So, whether as technology or currency, Bitcoin or other forms of crypto probably still have a long future ahead. This means that if you invest now, you might still be getting in on the ground floor. After all, some experts have predicted that Bitcoin may one day be worth as much as $100,000. According to leaked (and widely quoted) Citibank research, one industry insider estimates the digital currency would be worth more than $300,000 per coin by the end of 2021.

So, did you miss the early Bitcoin rush? Probably. Should you still invest in crypto?

The early years of Bitcoin trading were often restricted to a few platforms in mostly the Western and developed world. Information on where, what, and when to buy and sell was harder to find and the domain of the tech-savvy. If you weren't in that niche, finding out enough to understand and invest in Bitcoin was difficult. The situation today is very different. There are many more platforms to trade and buy bitcoin and other cryptocurrencies operating in literally every part of the world. Regardless of the part of the world you currently are in, you can purchase cryptocurrency with a secure internet connection and a few clicks on your smartphone.

While Bitcoin was a novelty, many more coins have come up with specific projects backing them, which has given more utility to

Bitcoin and thus increased its value. Global organizations such as banks who initially criticized Bitcoin have now adopted or are moving toward having Bitcoin as part of their portfolio. It would seem the future is indeed bright for cryptocurrency and Bitcoin. But it's not all roses.

Along with these returns have also come enormous risks. Between January 2017 and December 2017, bitcoin had an unprecedented boom going from below $1000 to an all-time high of $19,783 on December 17, 2017. Within a month, between January 6 and February 6, 2018, the price of Bitcoin dropped by nearly 65 percent. Following Bitcoin's crash, practically all other cryptocurrencies that had peaked between December 2017 and January 2018 followed suit. Cryptocurrencies had fallen 80% from their peak in January 2018, making the 2018 bitcoin crisis worse than the 78 percent drop experienced during the Dot-com bubble. Thousands of investors lost the money that they had invested during the boom.

More regulation means that crypto is more likely to become safer and more mainstream. Before you think crypto is already overcrowded, bear in mind that only about 4% of the world's population currently owns cryptocurrency.

You Didn't Miss the Train

More people are still becoming millionaires from their cryptocurrency investments. Bitcoin and cryptocurrency wouldn't be so popular now if people weren't still making lots of money from it. Let us give you an example. By November 2020, Bitcoin was trading in the $18000 price range. By November 2021, it was in the $56,000 range, having reached highs of $67,000 in early November 2021—over 300% growth. While the prices remain volatile, your money invested in November 2020 would have been doubled or tripled by now.

While no other coin might turn out to be another Bitcoin, there are a lot of possibilities. In fact, some other currencies have witnessed even more extraordinary growth in the past year than Bitcoin. Ethereum went from $567 in November 2020 to an incredible $4,057 in November 2021. The now infamous meme coin Doge went from $0.46 in December 2020 to a high of $30 in April 2021. Many people talk of the flippening, the potential moment when Ethereum passes Bitcoin as having the highest market cap.

In October 2021 alone, lots of crypto millionaires were minted by the rise in the price of the "meme coin" Shiba. These people became millionaires from having bought or owned a few dollars worth of the meme coin Shiba. And guess what? They didn't buy it in 2010 or 2011. They bought it as recently as 2020.

Blockchain, cryptocurrency, and Bitcoin have unleashed a universe of investment opportunities. You might have missed the initial Bitcoin rush, but we believe it's still early in the adoption of cryptocurrency, and there are many more gains to be had. Investing now could be a great asset in your journey toward financial freedom and beyond. We believe a small cryptocurrency investment could be an excellent investment for many people. But is it right for you? And how can you get involved? We'll go deeper into this later in the book.

Opportunities Abound

The only way to ensure you don't miss out is to explore the opportunity presented by the current times. Opportunities to invest in Bitcoin and crypto abound, perhaps even more than before. A few years ago, the only way to invest in cryptocurrency was to buy Bitcoin and wait for years for the prices to rise. A lot has changed.

There are more coins, more ways to use them, and in some cases, a lot more money to invest. One of the biggest reasons people balk at the prospect of cryptocurrency investment is that the idea of digital money can seem shrouded in mystery, almost as though this community is reserved exclusively for the ultra-smart and the tech geeks. In reality, this perception couldn't be more wrong. Cryptocurrency investment is for everyone, providing they understand it, just like real estate investments, stocks, and bonds.

While you may not know or understand how the computers that power the stock exchange work, you certainly can understand how to buy and trade stocks. The same goes for crypto. No one was born with an in-built knowledge of cryptocurrency, and before 2008, no one, not even the self-professed geeks, knew much about cryptocurrencies. This book will discuss cryptocurrencies and how to invest in them for beginners from every sphere of life. This brings us to the first rule of cryptocurrency trading and investing.

Remember This Cryptocurrency Rule

While crypto is not just for the super-smart pros, it is still somewhat complicated and needs explaining, sometimes repeatedly. This is why the number one rule is this: don't invest in cryptocurrency until you understand it. This applies to practically any other investment opportunity, but it is vital in cryptocurrency investing for several good reasons. For one, this type of money is unlike our traditional currency. It is not controlled by any central authority, and so different rules apply. Also, cryptocurrency can bestow great returns and financial freedom, but it can be quite risky if you are ill-informed, and you might end up losing all your money.

There are lots of crypto millionaires, but many have lost money. A lot of these people never bothered to learn how to invest in crypto. Many were greedy for quick returns, and, driven by the Fear Of Missing Out (FOMO; this is the first of many Crypto jargons we are going to explain in this book), they jumped right in.

Before you invest in cryptocurrencies, the most crucial question you should ask yourself is why you're doing it. There are a lot of investment opportunities available. Many of these are less volatile than cryptocurrencies. Why Cryptocurrency? Are you interested in cryptocurrency solely because of the Bitcoin craze's current popularity? Is there a specific reason you are investing in a particular coin? The answers to these questions depend on your financial objectives, which determine how much research you do and the kind of cryptocurrency investments you make.

The primary purpose of this book is to get you started on your journey to financial freedom through crypto investing, depending on your financial objectives and where you are in your current situation. We are still early in the crypto investing space, and many describe it as the wild wild west. Warren Buffet once said that the first rule of investments is never to lose money. The second rule is never to forget rule No 1. The fact that you are reading this book means you recognize the need to understand crypto before diving in with both feet.

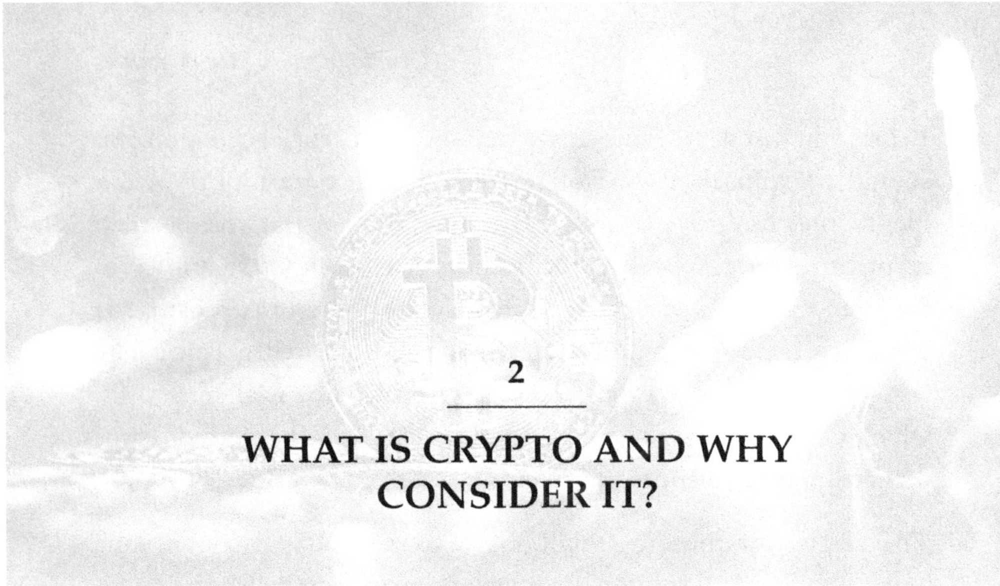

2

WHAT IS CRYPTO AND WHY CONSIDER IT?

What Is Cryptocurrency?

The term "cryptocurrency" is derived from two words: "cryptography" and "currency." Let's start with a definition of common currencies. Currency is any form of money that is used as a medium of exchange, particularly circulating paper money. Currencies act as an "economic buffer," allowing individuals to convert their labor into something that holds its value and can be converted back into products or other services at a later time.

For its part, think of cryptography as the process of converting plain text to incomprehensible text and vice versa. Consider how spies communicate through codes to ensure that the information they transmit cannot be read by anybody other than the intended recipient. Well, modern encryption mirrors this and emphasizes confidentiality—nobody can read data, data can't be modified, and only the sender and receiver may authenticate each other.

In this way, cryptocurrency is a type of digital money. It is a digital means of exchanging value (just like traditional currencies) that uses encryption to keep transactions safe. Attempts to create this type of money have been made for many years without success. These past failures happened because, with the introduction of digital money came the problem of 'double-spending.'

Let's illustrate this with an example. Say you have a $10 bill. You can use this to buy a cup of coffee, for instance, but once you do, you would be unable to re-use that same $10 bill to buy anything else. With past digital currencies, it was possible to make a purchase with some part of your virtual currency, send a duplicate of that money to the merchant you bought the product from, and still retain your original digital currency. Put differently, you could re-spend the exact same money twice.

Bitcoin was the very first cryptocurrency to succeed because it solved this problem. To achieve this, it relied on a technology which works as a distributed ledger of all transactions on the Bitcoin network. This technology is known as the 'blockchain,' which we'll discuss in greater detail in the next chapter of this book. Each transaction is carefully verified by individuals known as 'miners.' Users are unable to spend the same bitcoin twice because by looking at the receipts of their past transactions, these miners can tell when a user is attempting to cheat the system by double-spending. This and many more features of cryptocurrency guarantees security and is one of the major reasons that the world is excited about cryptocurrency.

WHAT'S SO SPECIAL ABOUT CRYPTO?

What's the big deal with Bitcoin if it's merely a way to buy items online? What distinguishes it from your credit card? Well, cryptocurrency is unusual in that it is a whole new type of currency. It exists to correct several existing flaws in our present monetary system. As a result, it is superior to our traditional currency, and someday might end up completely replacing it. Let's highlight a few of the advantages of cryptocurrency.

Decentralization

Cryptocurrency is not issued by any central government or authority. Decentralization is the key to its power. This means there is no single record keeper or ledger in the cryptocurrency system. The blockchain technology upon which cryptocurrency is based allows for this decentralization. With currencies that run on a centralized ledger, human manipulation and corruption are possible (i.e., when a single organization manages the transaction records, such as a National Central Bank). With cryptocurrency, the records are decentralised and shared amongst many ledgers, essentially eliminating the need for Central Banks. This type of ledger lies at the basis of cryptocurrency, which leads us to the second reason it's worth paying attention to.

Security

It's almost impossible to forge cryptocurrency or to double spend. The blockchain ledger is distributed globally at the same time, across thousands, or in the case of Ethereum and Bitcoin, millions of computers, thus guaranteeing security and transparency. Imagine if someone intended to fake a single data block on a chain from the blockchain network. In that situation, they would have to change all of the blocks from a certain point in time forward and update all of the computers that have copies of the blockchain ledger. Although theoretically plausible, the amount of power and money required to pull it off is nearly impossible.

Privacy

Transactions with cryptocurrency are (mostly) private. Traditional government-issued currencies allow you to conduct private transactions or make payments in person using actual currency. Paper, metal, cloth, and plastic currencies account for a small percentage of the total money in circulation. These monies are referred to as fiat currencies because they are issued and controlled by a central government (Dollar, Euro, Yen) and are not backed by a physical asset. Large cash withdrawals are promptly detected and investigated by the central authority, such as governments and banking system authorities. Cryptocurrency is a unique concept. To track the exchange between two persons or firms, you need an advanced understanding of various math concepts. While the ledger or list of transactions may be viewed by anybody in the world, the people who exchange cryptocurrencies are more private. Cryptocurrencies are held electronically in things known as 'digital wallets.' The owner of the cryptocurrency also owns a private key to his wallet without which even he would be unable to access his crypto assets.

Anti-Inflationary

Since our governments (through our central banks) print as much money as they want, fiat currencies (such as dollars and euros) have an endless supply. Central banks routinely change the value of their countries' currencies as part of their economic goals. The majority of countries manipulate their currencies in order to inflate them over time. Fiat currencies fall in value over time because they are inherently inflationary. As a result, holders of fiat currencies may pay the expense of depreciation as well as the risk of currency manipulation. In contrast, some cryptocurrencies have a finite and predetermined supply that is built into the underlying algorithm when the cryptocurrency is created. Bitcoin, for example, has a limited quantity of 21 million coins, after which no more coins may be created. Limited supply makes Bitcoin inherently deflationary and avoids losing value over time. Adding to this is the fact that Bitcoin goes missing every year.

A BRIEF HISTORY OF CRYPTOCURRENCY

Cryptocurrency existed as a theoretical concept long before the first digital alternative currencies were actually created. Early cryptocurrency proponents shared the ambition for using cutting-edge mathematic and computer science ideas to address what they saw as the practical and physical flaws of "conventional" fiat currencies.

The technical underpinnings of cryptocurrency extend to the early 1980s, when David Chaum, an American cryptographer, created a "blinding" method still used in modern web-based encryption. This method enabled parties to communicate secure, unalterable information, setting the framework for future electronic cash transfers.

A white paper on b-money—a virtual currency design that featured many of the essential components of modern cryptocurrencies, such as advanced anonymity safeguards and decentralization—was published about 15 years later by an accomplished software developer named Wei Dai. Regrettably, b-money was never used as a medium of exchange.

In the late 1990s and early 2000s, more traditional digital financial intermediaries appeared. These included PayPal, which gained Tesla inventor and notable cryptocurrency enthusiast Elon Musk his first fortune. Paypal proved to be a forerunner in today's mobile payment technologies.

There was no true cryptocurrency until the late 2000s when Bitcoin appeared on the market. Bitcoin is widely regarded as the first modern cryptocurrency. It was the first publicly traded digital asset to combine the key features of decentralized governance, user privacy, blockchain-based record-keeping, and built-in scarcity. In a white paper published in 2008, Satoshi Nakamoto, (whose actual identity is still unknown) presented it for the first time. Satoshi Nakamoto released Bitcoin to the broader public in early 2009, and a small group of fervent supporters began exchanging and mining the money. Within two years, other cryptocurrencies such as Litecoin had emerged as copycats of Bitcoin and were also growing popular. The first public Bitcoin exchanges appeared around the same time. WordPress became the first major platform to accept Bitcoin payments in late 2012. Others followed, including Newegg.com, Expedia, and Microsoft.

Currently, many companies and merchants now regard Bitcoin as a legitimate currency for transactions. Along with Bitcoin, other cryptocurrencies are gaining ground. Despite the fact that few cryptocurrencies other than Bitcoin are generally accepted for merchant payments, users can easily exchange their other coins for normal currencies such as the dollar. This offers vital liquidity and flexibility, which has made Bitcoin even more popular. In 2021, even traditional institutions, including banks such as JP Morgan, are now actively looking for ways to get involved.

WHO CONTROLS CRYPTOCURRENCY?

Bitcoin and the many other cryptocurrencies are decentralized. What exactly does this mean? In essence, there is no central body or government that controls the issuance of bitcoin tokens. Transactions are carried out on a peer-to-peer basis. Put differently, crypto transactions take place, are authenticated and recorded across the blockchain network without the involvement of any third party such as a bank. Essentially, cryptocurrencies are controlled by the people who use them. Transactions can be made through exchanges or directly through your cryptocurrency wallet. Since they are not the issuing authority and transactions are peer-to-peer, the government cannot directly control or regulate cryptocurrencies.

Does this mean the government is powerless in the face of cryptocurrency regulations? Not really. Various world governments have enacted legislation to regulate access to Bitcoin and cryptocurrencies via other ways. For example, in China, the government has been able to control and manage cryptocurrencies through land use and utility legislation. They've also been successful in shutting down cryptocurrency exchanges and preventing them from operating in the country. A similar, albeit softer, strategy has been taken in the United States. The Securities and Exchange Commission (SEC) has been able to impose restrictions on ICOs (initial coin offerings), thereby prohibiting corporations from issuing cryptocurrency.

Why You May Have Doubts

I can't control it. Why should I invest in something I can't control?

It is natural to have doubts about cryptocurrency, especially when new to it. A lot of these doubts come from misconceptions about cryptocurrency. One of these is about control. In reality, as long as you safeguard your digital wallet and keys, you have total control over your cryptocurrency. This may also be a good time to remind you that you do not control the dollar or the stock exchange.

Is Bitcoin Money?

In the past few years, this has been one of the raging arguments about Bitcoin. To answer this question, let's briefly discuss the qualities of money to better understand if bitcoin also serves these functions. Economists say that money performs three functions. It serves as:

- A unit of account: People can measure their wealth using it as a metric.
- A medium of exchange: People use it to conduct financial transactions and trade.
- A store of value: People can use it to keep their wealth.

This is often broken down to mean that money must be fungible, portable, durable, acceptable, divisible, uniform, and rare, to name a few characteristics. The question then is, does bitcoin fulfil these criteria? The answer at present is—yes.

Fungible: Because all Bitcoins are interchangeable, one Bitcoin can be replaced for another.

Portable: Bitcoin is the most portable form of money yet devised. One can keep as much bitcoin as they desire on a USB drive or memorize a set of 24 words (known as a "seed phrase") that act as the key to their currency.

Durable: Bitcoin is based on an immutable ledger that exists on the internet. To keep one's bitcoin, one can use external wallets. Bitcoin will remain in one's ownership indefinitely as long as they have access to their wallet or seed phrase.

Acceptable: Bitcoin is borderless and permissionless, which means a central authority or a government cannot stop it. The network is open to anyone globally, making it the most widely accepted currency in history. It is not even necessary to identify oneself. Although bitcoin is still in its early stages of acceptance, this should not be confused with its intrinsic features.

Uniform: All bitcoins are the same and are 100% provable via code on the blockchain. The 'double spend' problem is solved by Bitcoin, which implies that independent validators on the network can check what is and isn't a bitcoin. Bitcoin is impossible to forge.

Divisible: Bitcoin is easily divisible, which eliminates one of gold's difficulties (which is why silver was typically used instead). One bitcoin can be divided into 100,000,000 parts (called Satoshi's after Satoshi Nakomoto, the creator of Bitcoin). If necessary, this limit can be broken down even further, making bitcoin the most divisible currency in history.

Store of Value: Something must be naturally rare in order to be a store of value. The number of bitcoins available is limited to 21 million. Bitcoin will never be issued again. It is the world's most valuable currency with one bitcoin exchanging for as high as sixty thousand dollars in 2021.

TYPES AND CATEGORIES OF CRYPTOCURRENCY

Cryptocurrencies generally fall into one of two categories:

• Cryptocurrencies, such as Bitcoin and Altcoins (non-Bitcoin cryptocurrencies).

• Tokens, which are programmable assets that exist within a platform's blockchain.

Although many people use the terms crypto, coins, and tokens interchangeably, it's critical to understand how they differ in order to grasp the basics of cryptocurrencies. Coins and tokens are both types of cryptocurrency, although they serve different purposes.

Coins are designed to be used as a kind of currency and are created on their own blockchain. Ether (ETH), for example, is a cryptocurrency built on the Ethereum network. Bitcoin and AltCoins are the two types of coins that generally exist.

What Are Altcoins and Tokens?

The term "altcoin" refers to any blockchain-based cryptocurrency that isn't bitcoin. "Altcoin" was coined as a shorthand for "alternative to Bitcoin." The vast majority of altcoins were created to improve on bitcoin in some way. Litecoin and Ethereum are two instances of altcoins. Despite the fact that most altcoins are based on the same basic architecture as bitcoin and share some of its qualities, each one has its own set of benefits for investors. Some altcoins utilize a different method for generating and validating transaction blocks. Some may include new features such as smart contracts, as well as benefits like lower price volatility or shorter processing times.

The term "crypto token" refers to a one-of-a-kind virtual currency token or the system and method for valuing cryptocurrencies. These tokens are fungible assets or utilities that have their own blockchains. Crypto tokens are frequently used to raise funds for crowd sales, but they can also be used to replace other items.

CRYPTOS OTHER THAN BITCOIN

While Bitcoin is by far the most popular cryptocurrency, there are a slew of others that are equally popular. The top seven cryptocurrencies by market capitalization at the time of writing are listed below. The total dollar worth of all the bitcoins or altcoins ever minted is known as market capitalization (or market cap). Since there are so many virtual currencies with such a wide range of prices, market capitalization aids in identifying the most valuable. It's worth noting that the blockchain platform's name may differ from the digital currency's.

Ethereum (ETH)

Ethereum, like Bitcoin, is a blockchain network, but it was built as a programmable blockchain, which means it wasn't built to support a currency, but to allow users to create, publish, monetize, and use decentralized apps (dApps). Ether (ETH), the Ethereum native currency, was designed as a method of payment on the Ethereum network. In September 2021, Ether was the second most popular virtual money, after Bitcoin. However, unlike Bitcoin, there is no limit to the number of ETHs that can be created.

Cardano(ADA)

Cardano is a third-generation blockchain platform known for having a network that is more efficient and long-lasting than several other cryptocurrencies. This is owing to the fact that it does not require the vast amounts of electricity that Bitcoin, for instance, requires. Cardano's cryptocurrency, ADA, is named after Ada Lovelace, a 19th-century mathematician.

Binance Coin (BNB)

Binance Coin (BNB) is a cryptocurrency token designed to be used as a medium of exchange on Binance, one of the largest cryptocurrency exchanges in the world. It was originally built on the Ethereum blockchain, but now runs on Binance's proprietary blockchain technology. BNB was created in 2017 as a utility token to help traders save money on Binance trading fees, but now it can also be used for anything from payments to booking travel, entertainment, internet services, and even financial services. BNB had a total supply of 200 million tokens, almost half of which were made available to investors during the Initial Coin Offering (ICO)

Tether

Tether was the first cryptocurrency to be touted as a "stablecoin," a type of cryptocurrency that is backed by fiat cash. The tether's value is determined by a fiat currency, in this example, the US dollar. Tether, like other stablecoins, is designed to provide users with stability, transparency, and lower transaction fees. Tether, unlike several cryptocurrencies, is not a speculative investment; rather, it can be utilized by investors who want to escape the crypto market's severe volatility. Tethers accounted for 57 percent of bitcoin trading as of February 2021.

Solana (SOL)

Solana is a blockchain platform that produces the Sol cryptocurrency. The Sol, one of the more volatile currencies in recent years, was trading at around $191.00 on September 10, 2021, compared to

$3.42 a year before. What accounts for its increasing presence in the cryptosphere?

Solana has made significant progress in decentralized finance (also known as Devi) and, in particular, smart contract technology, which consists of programs that run on the platform according to predetermined criteria (like paper contracts, but without the middlemen). Solana was also behind the August 2021 launch of the "Degenerate Ape Academy," a non-fungible token (NFT).

Dogecoin (DOGE)

Dogecoin (pronounced dohj-coin) was actually created as a joke back in 2013 to mock Bitcoin. Its growth was further spurred on by the novelty of cryptocurrency and it quickly caught on. Dogecoin is an altcoin that functions similarly to Bitcoin and Ethereum in that it is based on a blockchain network and uses a proof-of-work (PoW) method. However, there is no limit to the quantity of coins that can be mined (versus the 21 million-coin cap on Bitcoin).

Dogecoin has also been linked to several high-profile crypto events, such as when investors contributed the equivalent of nearly $30,000 in Dogecoin to help send the Jamaican bobsled squad to the 2014 Winter Olympics. The currency drew a lot of interest and a significant quantity of money. Elon Musk tweeted in April 2019 that he thought Dogecoin was a good idea, which helped to enhance Dogecoin's status as a viable cryptocurrency. Despite being one of the most valuable currencies in terms of market capitalization, it trades at one of the lowest prices: around 24 cents as of September 10, 2021.

WHY PRICES FLUCTUATE

At its most fundamental level, cryptocurrency prices are determined by the tenets of supply and demand, one of the most basic economic notions. Prices will fall if supply is great and demand is low. On the other hand, if demand is high but supply is scarce, prices will skyrocket. Remember that crypto-coins have a finite supply; for example, Bitcoin has a supply capacity of 21 million, which means there can only be 21 million of them in the world. Bitcoin's price will rise once all of the coins are mined and people stop trading.

Publicity also influences supply and demand. If a currency receives positive feedback and media attention, it begins to be exchanged in greater quantities, resulting in a price increase and vice versa. Such minor elements have such a large impact on cryptocurrency prices because crypto is still a relatively new market. Daily cryptocurrency trade is estimated to be worth around $14 billion, while daily forex trading is worth nearly $5 trillion. So, despite the hoopla, cryptocurrency is still in its infancy (which is a good thing for you).

CHALLENGES OF CRYPTO INVESTING

Crypto Hype Risk

It's tempting to get carried away by cryptocurrency's promise of financial freedom. Cryptocurrency hype, on the other hand, isn't necessarily positive. The fact that many individuals have no idea what they're investing in is the fundamental cause for the excitement surrounding cryptos. As a result, they wind up listening to the crowd instead. People begin to pull back once they realize what they've bought in, which can lead to a price crash.

Security Risk

Have you heard of crypto scams, hackings, and cyber theft? Since Bitcoin's creation in 2009, these have been a frequent topic in the cryptocurrency industry. And, with each scandal, the value of cryptocurrencies is harmed, albeit only temporarily. As a result, you must take safety precautions at every stage of your bitcoin investment strategy.

Volatility Risk

Volatility risk refers to the danger of unanticipated market changes. Volatility might be beneficial, but it can also take you off guard at times. The bitcoin market, like any other market, might go in the opposite direction of what you predict. If you are not prepared for market volatility, you risk losing the money you have invested.

Vanishing Risk

There are hundreds of different cryptocurrencies available right now. Every day, more and more cryptocurrencies are introduced. Many of these cryptocurrencies may vanish in ten years, while others may thrive. Consider the dot-com bubble as an example of vanishing danger. Many people worldwide dreamed up enterprises based on the internet's growth in the late 1990s. Some, like Amazon and eBay, have been successful in conquering the world. Many more went down in flames. Many of the burgeoning cryptocurrencies cropping up left and right are doomed to fail.

Scalability

Scalability is one of the most important issues that anyone interested in bitcoin as an investment option has to worry about. Despite the tremendous growth in the number of currencies and the number of people eager to adopt crypto, the numbers are still low when compared to credit and cash transactions.

Absence of Regulations

There are many who believe that the lack of a regulatory framework makes investing in cryptocurrency risky. Cryptocurrency might be a great investment if the technology is mastered and the difficulties handled. Even so, without government supervision, the investment platform may be extremely dangerous. There are certain risks involved as well, although they are largely logistical.

YOU NEED A PLAN: FEEL SAFE, PLAY SAFE

Remember that old adage that goes, "If you fail to plan, you plan to fail?" Well, it is true. Having a plan from the start is one of the best methods to increase your chances of success when investing in cryptocurrency. It's like having a compass or a map when traveling through unfamiliar territories. This way, when confronted with the volatility of crypto, you'll know exactly what to do. Let's have a look at how to make a workable plan.

How To Create a Cryptocurrency Investment Plan

Developing a bitcoin investment strategy isn't as difficult as you would imagine. In actuality, an investment plan's basics are the same across asset classes. According to universal concepts, operating procedures are required to keep your investments in check and on track. Otherwise, you risk making emotional rather than logical decisions.

Here's a three-step procedure for building an investing strategy if you want to invest in cryptocurrencies properly.

1. Allocate Funds

To begin, set aside a portion of your investable savings for this asset class. You shouldn't put all of your money into cryptos, just as you shouldn't put all of your money into equities. Your money will be more vulnerable to risk. Only invest in crypto what you are prepared to lose.

Cryptocurrencies are commonly viewed as risky and volatile investments, with prices that can fluctuate dramatically, resulting in huge gains or devastating losses. While it varies depending on who you ask, it's widely agreed that speculative investments should not account for more than 5–10% of a portfolio (depending on your risk preferences and investment goals). For example, if you have $20,000 to invest, you could put $1000 to $2,000 into cryptocurrencies based on those percentages.

2. Research Coins

Once you've decided how much you're going to invest, it's time to do your own research and assess various coins. Start by looking at cryptocurrency exchanges like Coinbase or Binance to get a sense of what's available. These sites show long lists of cryptocurrencies that you may sort by price, price movements, market capitalization, and other factors. If you're interested in smaller cryptos, you can use online resources like coinmarketcap.com to find markets where these can be bought and traded.

Cryptocurrencies usually have a specific function and are designed to address problems. So, the first thing you should learn about a coin is what problem(s) it solves. Most coins have websites that explain what they are and how they work, so start there.

Currencies are not like firms because they don't have tangible assets or operations to assess. If a new cryptocurrency is not bringing anything new to the market in terms of value and solutions, it's unlikely to be a good investment. Furthermore, because cryptocurrencies are not regulated in the same way that publicly listed firms are, there is no standardized reporting or disclosure standard. On the other hand, many coin producers provide thorough information about their currencies through whitepapers, detailed essays that assist users in comprehending their coin's underlying technology.

While knowing what you're buying is crucial, you don't need to learn hundreds of pages of coding and decentralized jargon. Concentrate on the fundamentals of a cryptocurrency that you can learn about, such as:

- The developers and management team (which isn't always open to the public) who are in charge.
- Supply, market capitalization, and volume are three metrics to consider.
- Research on social media to get an idea of the strength and size of the community.

3. Create An Exit Strategy

Exit strategies keep you from selling at the wrong time or at the incorrect price. Consider the following questions:

- What are you hoping to achieve with these investments? (For example, to fund a trip, to accumulate wealth, and so on.)
- How long do you think you'll be able to hold out?
- When will you require these monies, if at all?
- What do you want to gain from this investment?
- What level of receptivity do you have to volatility?
- How would you react if the value of your coins plummeted by half?

These questions will assist you in determining your departure plan based on Time and Price. The first three questions will assist you in determining a time frame for your cryptocurrency investments. If your aim is immediate, such as a planned trip, you know you're dealing with a short-term situation and are more vulnerable to price fluctuations. If your goal is to grow money over time, you won't have to worry as much about daily volatility. Determining this ahead of time can help you develop a mentality that will guide your activities.

The fourth question aids in the selection of appropriate price objectives. You can reverse engineer your price targets. For example, if you're investing $1,000 in cryptos with the intention of making $5,000. Let's imagine you buy one hundred $10 coins to keep things simple. In that situation, you'd need your coin's price to rise to $50 in order to reach your $5,000 investment target ($50 price x 100 coins). In this instance, your pricing goal would be $50.

3

BLOCKCHAIN BREAKDOWN

Why You Should Understand Blockchain

We mentioned blockchain technology briefly in the previous chapter of this book, but what is it? How does it really work, and why should you care about it all? According to the most recent world statistics, about 0.5 percent of the world's population uses blockchain. By comparison, the internet is used by around 50% of the world's population or some 3.77 billion people. Despite these low figures, the blockchain network is widely believed to have unlimited potential to make modern life much better. Experts believe that blockchain has the potential to transform the world even more than the internet did. This is a massive opportunity for you to understand this incredible technology, get ahead of the rest of the population, and stay ahead.

One of the fascinating features of blockchain is that, with its Distributed Ledger Technology (DLT), it creates a new type of market infrastructure that sits on top of and connects with all existing systems and procedures. As a result, it can be applied or used in practically any area, including finance, food supply chains, technology, the health sector, fashion, and even government. This means that, regardless of your business, a fundamental understanding of blockchain is essential if you want to be relevant in the near future.

But, above all, blockchain should be studied for investment purposes. Since blockchain is the underlying technology of cryptocurrencies, you'll be able to make smarter investments and trades if you can firmly grasp its concepts. This also offers the option to invest in the finest coins and tokens as well as new companies using blockchain technology. Remember Rule #1: Never invest in cryptocurrency unless you understand it, including knowing about blockchain. Before investing your funds in cryptocurrencies, let's dive in and learn all about the technology behind them below.

All About Blockchain

Let's assume you live in a small town called Cryptodora, where various records are generated and kept in the Town City Hall. These include land records and population records. As a citizen, you'll be making regular tax payments to the town coffers. This, of course, is to be used for the management and development of the whole town. A ledger would normally be used to keep track of your payments. The town's mayor and perhaps the town's accountant will be responsible for this ledger and the other records. Because there is only one ledger and one or two custodians now, it is easy to manipulate the records.

Indeed, you are all aware of what occurred at the neighboring town Cryptohype—the mayor and the accountant continued to steal money and make hidden alterations to the ledgers, resulting in the town losing money and going bankrupt. The mayor even altered estate records to sell some of the town's lands to himself. On the other hand, you folks have a wonderful idea: each citizen will have their own ledger, where all records, tax payments, and expenses will be entered into everyone's ledger simultaneously.

To steal and cover their tracks, the mayor and accountant would have to go to everyone's residence and change the records one by one, which would be nearly impossible. This is the height of transparency. This brilliant system you developed for your town is called a Distributed Ledger System. A Distributed Ledger Technology (DLT) or blockchain is a system in which everyone has a ledger and retains records at the same time, and can observe any changes at the same time. This ledger file is not kept in one company's records on a central server. Instead, the ledger file is spread globally and saved on personal computers that are all utilized to store data and execute calculations.

Blockchain is a data storage system that makes it difficult or impossible to change, hack, or manipulate the data. A blockchain is essentially a digital ledger of transactions that is duplicated and distributed across the network of computers that make up the blockchain. Each block on the chain comprises a number of transactions, and whenever a new transaction takes place on the blockchain, each participant updates the ledger. This means that if a single block in a chain was modified, it would be immediately apparent. Hackers would have to alter every block in the chain across all distributed versions of the chain if they wanted to corrupt a blockchain system.

How Does It Work?

Let's take the most well-known application of blockchain, Bitcoin, as an example of how it works. As we have discussed, bitcoin is a digital currency, just like any other national currency. Bitcoin was built using the blockchain distributed ledger system, a file that keeps track of all transactions and keeps track of how many bitcoins each user possesses.

Let us continue our town example. Now your smart town of Cryptodora has developed a system to ensure that town records can't be altered. Some young high school kids decide to go further. Why don't you use this system to create a payment system that everyone can monitor? This currency is called bitcoin.

When the mayor wants to pay the Waste Management Contractor 5 bitcoins, they will send a message to all nodes (in this case, citizens) specifying that the town's bitcoins should be lowered by 5 and Waste Management Contractor's be increased by 5. Each computer (citizen) will now get this data and update its copy of the town's and the contractor's bitcoin balances. This system effectively removes the need for a central record keeper (i.e., banks).

Blockchain allows everyone to view each other's transactions and removes the need to trust a person or organization. For instance, if the town estate records are built on a blockchain system, no one can change property records or defraud anyone by selling the same property twice. This system can be applied to various business and social life areas, which is why experts believe it is so revolutionary.

To ensure security and reliability, certain mathematical functions and codes are used. With Bitcoin, each wallet is safeguarded by a cryptographic mechanism that employs a unique and distinct pair of linked keys: a public and a private key. Each of these characteristics of blockchain technology leads to a particular benefit from its application.

It is upon this blockchain that Bitcoin and all cryptocurrencies are built.

Benefits of Blockchain

Let's talk about the advantages of blockchain technology.

1. *Transparency*: Transaction histories are more transparent than ever because of blockchain. All nodes in the network share a copy of the documentation because it is a distributed ledger. The data on a blockchain ledger is open

to the public and may be viewed by anybody. Everyone in the network can notice the change and the updated record if a transaction history changes. As a result, everyone has access to all currency exchange information.

2. *Security*: By all accounts, blockchain outperforms any other record-keeping system in terms of security. A blockchain network's shared transaction documentation can only be updated and/or amended with consensus. The information is only updated if everyone or a majority of nodes agree to do so. Furthermore, once a transaction is approved, it is encrypted and linked to the preceding one. As a result, no single person or party has the power to change a record. Because blockchain is decentralized, no one has the authority to update records at their leisure. Blockchain may be used to impose tight security in any area that has a crucial requirement to protect sensitive data, such as governments, healthcare, financial services, and so on.
3. *Efficiency*: Completing a transaction via traditional paperwork methods is time-consuming and prone to human mistakes because it requires third-party mediation. These archaic processes can be streamlined and disciplined with blockchain, removing the possibility of errors and making trading more efficient and faster. Parties do not have to retain various records because there is only one ledger, resulting in significantly less clutter. It's also easier to build trust when everyone has access to the same information. Settlements can also be made smooth and painless without the use of intermediaries.
4. *Traceability*: It can be challenging to track things back to their source in complex supply chains. However, with blockchain, all goods trades are recorded, giving you an audit trail to figure out where a specific asset comes from. You'll also learn about every stop the goods made along the

way, and this level of product tracking can aid in verifying authenticity and preventing fraud.

5. *Cost Savings*: Because blockchain eliminates the need for third parties and intermediaries, it saves organizations a lot of money. You don't need anyone else to set the norms and policies of exchange if you can trust your trade partner. Everyone can see a single immutable version of the ledger, which reduces the cost and time spent on documentation and changes.

PART II

TRADING AND INVESTING IN CRYPTOCURRENCY

4

HOW AND WHY TO INVEST

WHY INVEST IN CRYTPO?

We have looked at cryptocurrencies and the enormous changes they bring to the world. Cryptocurrencies are valid as technological marvels and are disrupting modern finance. The big question is should you invest in crypto? Here are some reasons you should invest.

1. Cryptocurrencies Have Revolutionised Our World

In earlier chapters, we discussed the revolutionary impact of cryptocurrencies. For this reason, many people believe that it is a smart investment choice. Cryptocurrency appears to have a promising future.

While we all know that cryptocurrencies are quite volatile, investing in them may be a safer and more promising option than other assets. For example, Bitcoin's history is tumultuous, and it has been declared lost on several occasions. Bitcoin achieved fresh all-time highs of

$20,000 in 2017, then plummeted below $5,000 in 2018. However, Bitcoin has weathered the storm and continues to thrive, and investors are optimistic about its future.

2. A Hedge Against Inflation

Inflation remains a bane in the current monetary systems. This is because the issuing governments have the power to print more currency whenever they choose. With most cryptocurrencies, this is impossible as they often have a predetermined supply that is encoded into the underlying algorithm at the time of creation. For Bitcoin, this supply stands at a maximum of 21 million coins, after which no more may be produced.

Others have a process called coin burning, a procedure through which cryptocurrency miners and developers remove a fraction of coins from circulation to regulate their price. Cryptocurrency can be a better store of value due to its limited supply. According to a report by JP Morgan, institutional investors are beginning to see Bitcoin as a better inflation hedge than gold.

3. Cryptocurrencies Have a High Liquidity

The cryptocurrency market is characterized by significant liquidity, implying that buying and selling cryptos is simple. For instance, Bitcoin is always in demand. According to statistics, the number of crypto wallets would have climbed to more than 80 million in 2021. In addition, investors and large corporations are willing to buy and trade cryptocurrencies. Cryptocurrency trading is now relatively easy to do.

4. Cryptocurrency Investment Has the Potential to Yield High Returns

Perhaps the most compelling motivation for people to invest in cryptocurrencies is the prospect of profit. Even though cryptocurrency trading is still in its infancy, it has the potential to outperform traditional assets, such as stocks. Due to its volatility, one trade may result in outsized profits.

At the same time, keep in mind that volatility means that traders might lose their entire investment in a matter of seconds. As a result, always think about the dangers! Due to the high demands of cryptocurrency investing, one of the first stages to success is to develop an efficient risk management strategy to limit losses.

5. Cryptocurrency Provides Freedom and Flexibility

Whether you invest in Ethereum or Doge coins, your crypto money is yours alone. Cryptocurrencies, as previously said, do not rely on banks, which charge expensive fees to retain your money. Furthermore, the crypto market is open 24 hours a day, seven days a week, so you don't have to worry about closing times; you can buy and sell whenever and however you want.

6. Diversification of Your Portfolio

Adding cryptocurrencies to your portfolio is a terrific way to diversify your holdings. What does it mean to diversify your portfolio? It's an excellent way to spread your investments and diversify your assets to reduce risk. You shouldn't put all your eggs in one basket, as the saying goes.

Cryptocurrency operates with a different dynamic from traditional investments such as stock. Therefore, investing in it provides a diversification in your portfolio that investors often desire.

7. Low Entry Threshold

While certain investments, such as equities and real estate, need significant initial capital, cryptocurrency offers a low entrance barrier. The good news is that many sites do not demand large sums of money to begin buying and trading cryptocurrency. With as little as $10, you can start investing in cryptocurrencies.

HOW TO INVEST AND MAKE MONEY WITH CRYPTO ASSETS

Buying Cryptocurrency

The most direct way is to simply buy cryptocurrency. This is the most popular form of crypto investment and the one this book focuses on. This involves choosing a currency and trading it on an exchange or holding it for the prices to rise. The rest of this book will focus on how you can invest in cryptocurrency by buying and trading it.

Invest in Crypto Exchange-Traded Funds (ETFs)

According to Investopedia, an exchange-traded fund (ETF) is a product that tracks the performance of a cryptocurrency, an index, a sector, a commodity, or other assets. Unlike conventional cryptocurrencies traded on crypto exchanges, crypto ETFs are purchased and sold on stock exchanges like regular equities.

ETFs that allow you to invest in many cryptocurrencies at once are in high demand. In October 2021, the Securities and Exchange Commission (SEC) approved the first US Crypto ETF. This is a viable crypto investment strategy that provides immediate diversification and is less risky than investing in individual cryptocurrencies.

While they offer less risk, Crypto ETFs have their downsides. Cryptocurrency ETFs do not make the investor a cryptocurrency owner. This imposes some restrictions on cryptocurrency use, such as the inability of shareholders to trade their Bitcoin for Ethereum and vice versa or benefit from the decentralized financial system that cryptocurrencies provide.

In addition, compared to ordinary ETFs, management fees for cryptocurrency ETFs are considered excessive. These fees can sometimes be as high as five times the cost of other more traditional ETFs.

Invest In Companies Connected to Cryptocurrency

You can buy stocks of companies connected to the crypto industry or invest in the development or use of crypto, a viable option if you prefer to invest in companies with actual products or services and are subject to regulatory control. This way, you enjoy better protection but still have exposure to the cryptocurrency industry. For example, you can invest in a company like Nvidia, a technological company that produces and sells graphics processing units (GPU; a high tech computer part), which are at the heart of cryptocurrency mining equipment.

As with any investment, make sure you assess your investment goals and current financial conditions before investing in cryptocurrencies or specific companies with considerable interest in them. Cryptocurrency has the potential to be incredibly volatile, which indicates you should invest with prudence and care.

Staking

Staking is analogous to a fixed-term deposit at a traditional bank. A person puts money in for a set period in exchange for prizes, bonuses, or interest. Staking cryptocurrency entails storing tokens in wallets for a set amount of time to participate in network governance.

Users receive a staking payment in exchange for keeping the currencies, confirming transactions, and contributing to the network's overall security. The staking incentive is calculated as a percentage of the total quantity of tokens locked in and wallets participating. Staking cryptocurrencies can often provide an annual percentage yield (APY), which is significantly higher than the interest paid by a regular bank. As usual, be careful of scams. Some projects offer wildly high returns, only for the organizers to disappear overnight with investors' money, pulling the rug out from under everybody (known as a rug pull). Like everything in investing, if it seems too good to be true, it probably is.

Yield Farming

This is a more advanced form of staking. In yield farming, the funds staked are used by the platform to increase liquidity. In essence, you're adding liquidity to a platform and collecting income due to doing so. It can be compared to putting regular currency money in a savings account. Savings account funds are employed in the bank's main liquidity pool. Banks use that pool to lend and provide money to clients. The concept is similar to yield farming, except you're donating to a lending platform rather than a bank.

Lending

If you already have Bitcoin or Ethereum in your wallet, you may put it to work and make some money by lending it out. The money is often lent out to other traders who require liquidity for their traders. Many peer-to-peer Bitcoin lending platforms allow you to do this while also providing you with a reasonable 2 to 8 percent return on your Bitcoin investment.

Play-To-Earn

Play to earn is an example of how cryptocurrency can affect all sectors. Play to earn combines the fun and fascination of gaming with the earning potentials of crypto. In Play-to-earn, users get control over in-game assets and enhance their worth by playing play-to-earn crypto games. They can receive tokens and coins as a reward for participating.

HOW TO CHOOSE A CRYPTOCURRENCY FOR INVESTMENT

When choosing a cryptocurrency to invest in, Bitcoin and Ether have the highest market capitalizations, accounting for about 70% of the total market. These two assets are as successful, secure, and well-established as cryptocurrencies can get, and they may be a good starting point for beginners. These two coins have already been discussed in Chapter Two.

Beyond Bitcoin and Ether are other coins with increased risk profiles. If you can bear the increased risk, there is a good possibility that you may invest in advanced crypto technologies and currencies that will one day lead the markets. These coins and tokens have come up to cater to various areas of the developing behemoth of blockchain technology and cryptocurrencies. The key here is to invest in a coin or token that will play an essential role in developing blockchain. You can think of Blockchain and Crypto as a developing city. Various businesses (coins and tokens) have sprung up. The businesses that will succeed are the ones that play critical roles in the development of the future of the city in critical areas such as transportation.

Here are some coin classifications to help you out.

Blockchain Competitors

As we have explained, the use of blockchain was pioneered by Bitcoin and Ether. However, the success of BTC and ETH has spawned a slew of competitors. Other coins that have built their own blockchain infrastructure are listed here. In the long run, these coins are projected to attain something akin to Bitcoin and Ether's success. Cardano (ADA), Polkadot (DOT), and Solana (SOL) are some examples.

Governance Tokens

Those in the know refer to crypto businesses that run on ethereum (or other blockchains) as "Dapps" which is short for "Decentralized applications." Many of these projects issue governance tokens, which allow token holders to vote on protocol decisions. Uniswap (UNI), Aave (AAVE), and Maker (MKR) are examples of these tokens.

Infrastructure Tokens

The decentralized nature of blockchain technology, according to computer experts, is the internet's future. People refer to this new internet paradigm as "Web 3.0," which relies on a combination of blockchain, media, and decentralized money (De-Fi). This Web 3.0 requires infrastructure in the form of IT businesses that can harness and store data and connect across different blockchains to function. Because this technology is crucial to the internet's future, their coins and tokens could be extremely valuable; think of early Microsoft or Apple stock. Chainlink (LINK), The Graph (GRT), and Filecoin (FIL) are examples of infrastructure tokens.

Exchange Tokens

We have discussed what tokens are. Now, exchange tokens are tokens offered by Crypto Exchange platforms issued to enable transactions on their platforms. Binance (BNB) is the most popular. Others are FTX Token (FTT) and Crypto.com Coin (CRO).

CRYPTO EXCHANGES VS. BROKERS

A cryptocurrency exchange is an online marketplace where traders can swap digital currencies. An exchange acts as an intermediary between buyers and sellers, allowing for fee-based trading. Cryptocurrency exchanges are used to buy cryptocurrency with fiat money, sell cryptocurrency for fiat money, or exchange cryptocurrencies—bitcoin for another cryptocurrency, for example. Crypto exchanges only deal with digital currencies, allowing traders to buy and sell them directly.

A cryptocurrency broker is a company that operates as an intermediary between a trader and the cryptocurrency market, making it easier to purchase, sell, and exchange cryptocurrencies. Trading crypto via a broker is more flexible and convenient than trading crypto on an exchange since it enables faster settlement.

One of the key differences between exchanges and brokers is that you do not own the cryptocurrency with brokers. This means that you may be unable to move your crypto holdings off the site. This may not appear to be a significant issue; knowledgeable crypto investors prefer to retain their funds in personal crypto wallets for added security.

How To Choose an Exchange

In the past few years, many crypto exchanges have become available. The five biggest platforms are:

Binance

Binance is one of the largest and most well-known cryptocurrency exchanges in the world. It's a popular choice among investors wishing to make significant purchases in the cryptocurrency market. Binance is a wonderful alternative for someone who needs more advanced charting than most other exchanges, as it offers over 50 different cryptocurrencies to trade.

Pros

- Purchases of $10,000 or more are made over the counter.
- Transaction fees are kept to a minimum.
- Has one of the most diverse cryptocurrency portfolios.

Cons

- Crypto-to-crypto pairs are limited.
- Identification, verification, and sign-up are all time-consuming processes.
- Not accessible from every state in the United States.

Coinbase

For almost a decade, Coinbase, founded in 2012, has been synonymous with cryptocurrency trading. It's now a tried-and-true path for individuals looking to get into the crypto world. Coinbase offers nearly 40 cryptocurrencies, a terrific wallet interface, and top-notch security.

Pros

- An easy-to-use interface for beginners.
- The exchange of bitcoins is simple and convenient.
- Purchases made directly.
- Compliant with US regulations.
- 98 percent of all cryptocurrencies are held in cold storage.

Cons

- Fees for transactions are increasing.
- Other exchanges have a larger assortment of coins.
- There aren't enough advanced crypto exchange features.

Crypto.com

Crypto.com, founded in 2018, allows users to spend cryptocurrencies using a prepaid Visa card. This makes Crypto.com an excellent choice for bitcoin investors who want to use cryptocurrencies regularly.

Pros

- On staked investments, token holders can earn income.
- There are no fees for deposits made through bank transfers.
- To purchase 100+ cryptocurrencies, you can use 20+ different fiat currencies.

Cons

- For beginners, this is not a suitable option.
- For new investors, it can be overwhelming.
- Access to certain functionalities is restricted.

Gemini

Gemini has developed to become a major industry powerhouse and one of the most regulated cryptocurrency exchanges in the world, with one of the most stringent New York BitLicenses. Apart from these, it has a number of other characteristics that make it the top crypto exchange in the United States with the most significant trading volume.

Pros

- The smartphone app for on-the-go trading (both iOS and Android).
- Cooperates with US regulators to ensure that best practices are followed.
- Trading volume is high.
- One of the most liquid exchange markets in the United States.

Cons

- Users using the mobile app are charged a commission fee and a convenience fee.
- Payments via credit or debit card are not accepted.
- There are fewer cryptos available.

Kraken

Kraken is one of the oldest crypto exchanges in the United States, founded as early as 2011. It offers a wide range of coins with low fees.

Pros

- Advanced traders may be interested in sophisticated trading features such as margin.
- High levels of security.

Cons

- The platform may be too complicated for beginners.

Make sure to do some research and choose wisely when looking for the best bitcoin trading exchanges. The security features, regulatory background, market accessibility, and trading platform should all play a role in your decision. Here are some things to think about.

Regulations: The first thing you should do is look into the exchange's regulatory compliance. Make sure you use a regulated exchange to protect yourself from scams and fraud. Because exchanges might be hacked or go bankrupt, your money and personal information security is critical when you register a trading account.

Credibility: Compared to established financial markets, the crypto market is still in its infancy. Try to locate an experienced exchange with strong credibility history, such as one with a good track record with licensed and regulated operations.

Reliable Customer Assistance: Another vital factor to consider when picking a cryptocurrency exchange is the availability of reliable customer support. An exchange's customer service should be open 24/7 to answer your questions and provide assistance whenever you need it. You can better understand the exchange's customer care tools and average wait times by contacting them.

Commissions and Fees: Take a close look at the exchange's account features and benefits. Each exchange offers a unique set of account benefits. Commissions and spread, simplicity of deposits and withdrawals, leverage and margin, and initial deposit requirements are four factors to consider when comparing account characteristics among exchanges.

Trading Platform: The trading platform is both your portal and your primary trading tool. As a result, you must ensure that an exchange's platform and software provide the necessary trading tools to execute trades smoothly. Opening a demo account is a simple way to test this one. It's a no-risk trial account that will allow you to get a feel for the exchanger's platform and services before committing to a permanent account.

Sign-Up Procedure: An exchange's sign-up process can reveal a lot about them. You can discern a good exchange from a bad one just by looking at their sign-up process—the better the exchange, the smoother the process. Check if the process is secure so that your personal information isn't exposed. Another factor to consider is the initial investment. Fake exchanges typically need traders to deposit a substantial sum of money to sign up. This is because they are more likely to defraud you. Instead, look for an exchange that has a minimal minimum deposit.

HOW TO BUY YOUR FIRST BITCOIN: A STEP-BY-STEP GUIDE

There are many platforms to buy bitcoin. Platforms like Paypal and Cashapp may be known to you even if you are unfamiliar with crypto. Others such as Binance and Coinbase are less popular unless you are interested in crypto.

For this step-by-step guide, we have chosen Binance as it is the biggest crypto exchange platform as of November 2021. You can do a little googling to know available platforms that are most convenient for you. Services will vary depending on your country of residence.

Step 1: Create your Binance account. Create an account using your email address or cell phone number and a secure password. Alternatively, you can open an account by downloading the Binance crypto trading software from the App Store or Google Play store. The registration process is quick and easy, despite the fact that it requires identity verification.

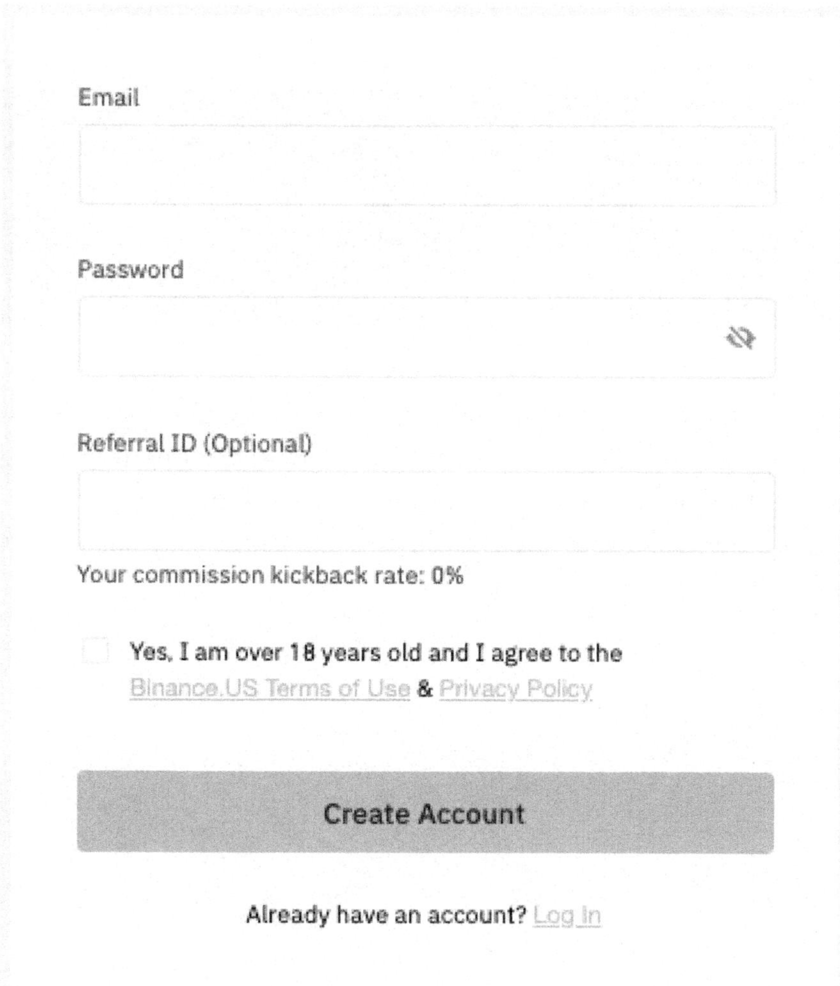

Step 2: Go to your Binance account and log in. Navigate to the upper-right corner of your screen once you've logged into the site. Locate the "Buy Now" button and hover your cursor over it. You can now buy crypto with up to five different methods: bank deposits, credit/debit cards, peer-to-peer trading, cash balance, and third-party payments. Click the "Credit/Debit Card" option as we're focusing on the most straightforward way to trade.

Step 3: Purchasing bitcoin on Binance using a credit or debit card is simple. The screen that appears after selecting the option mentioned above demonstrates this: you'll be taken to a website where you may choose the amount of money you wish to spend on your Binance BTC purchase.

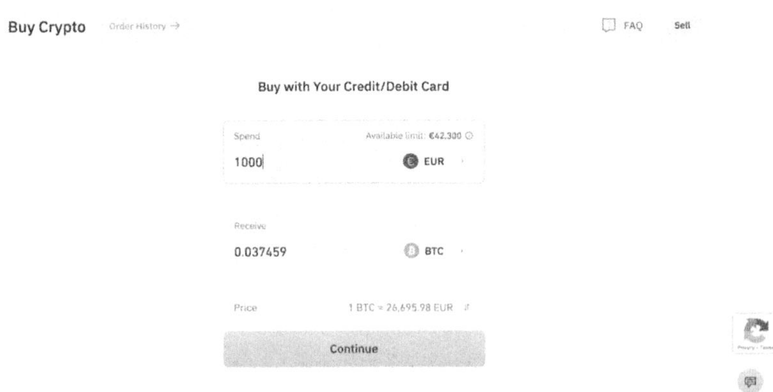

Step 4: Once you've decided how much money you want to spend, select "Buy." You'll be requested to verify your account (if you didn't do so during account registration) at this point in the shopping process. Click "Verify Now." If you are already verified, go straight to Step 6.

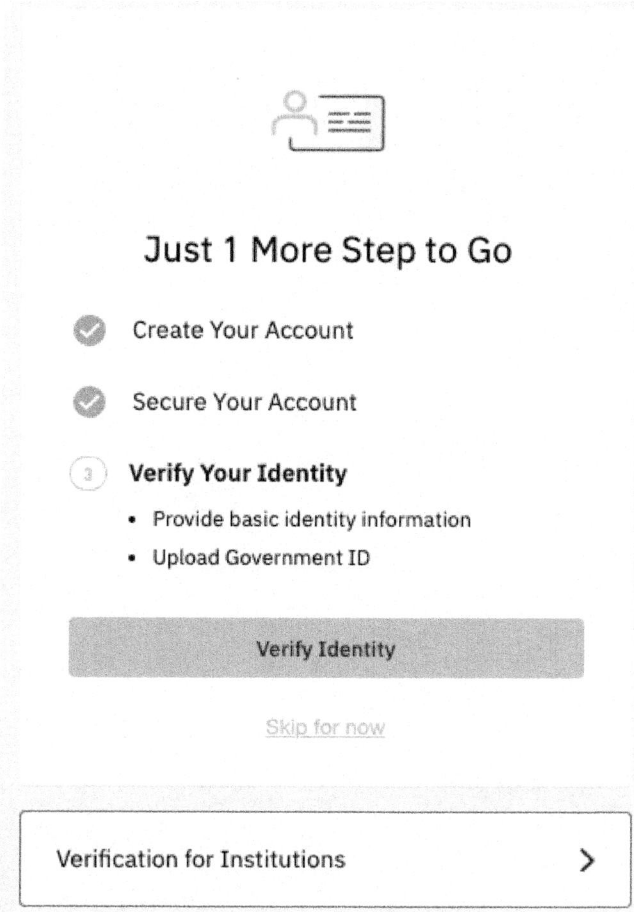

Step 5: When you get to the verification screen, you'll notice that you need to authenticate your identity with Binance before you can make your first trade. This entails entering your legal first and last names, birth date, and residential address, as well as submitting a photo of your ID and taking a selfie. This is all a pretty standard process for crypto exchange platforms.

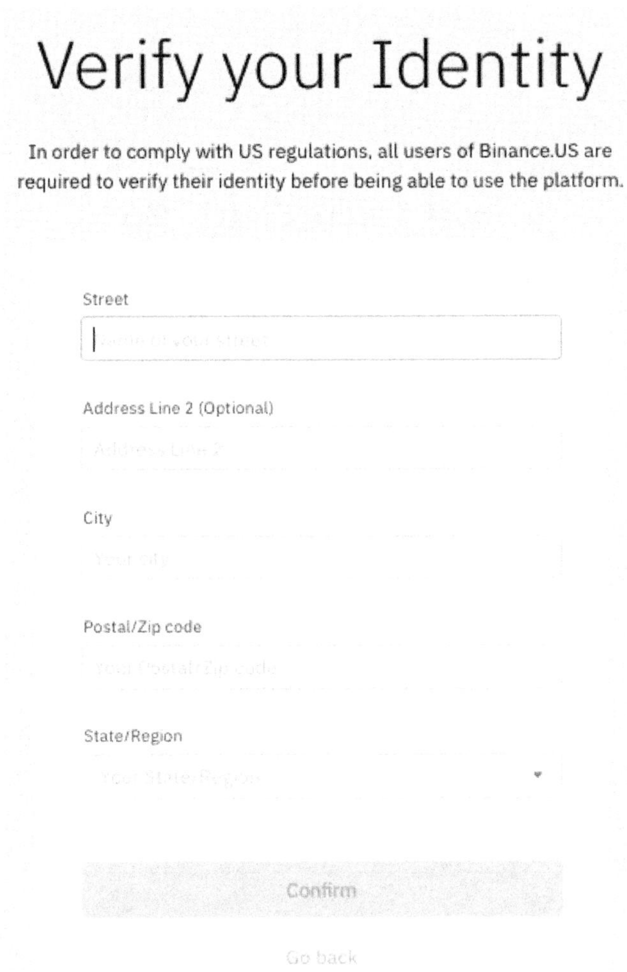

Step 6: After you've validated your account, you must confirm your payment information. This is because, with Binance, you may buy BTC using your credit or debit card.

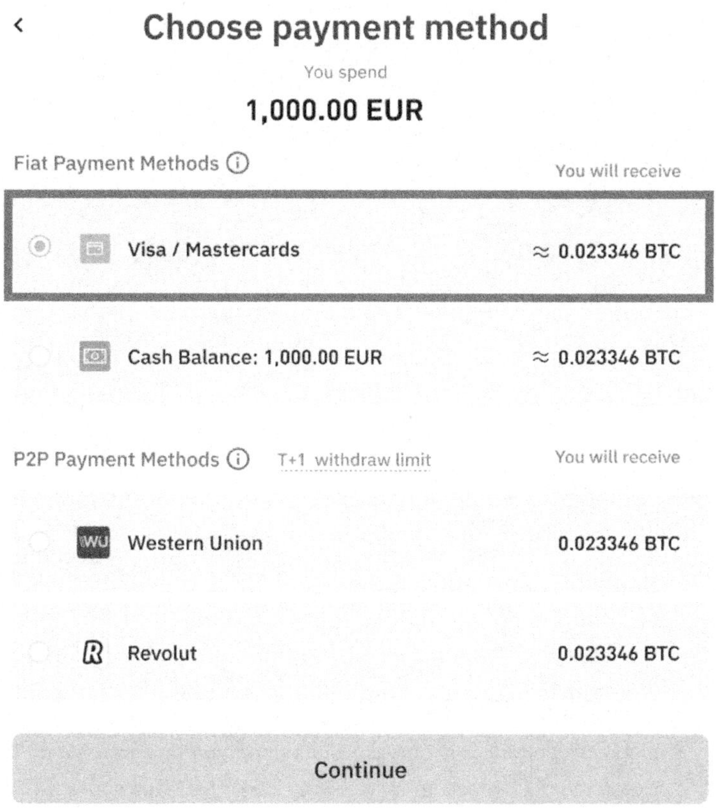

Step 7: Once you've done all of that, and you've selected the amounts of Binance BTC you want to buy as well as validated your account, all that's left is to review the order summary and confirm it!

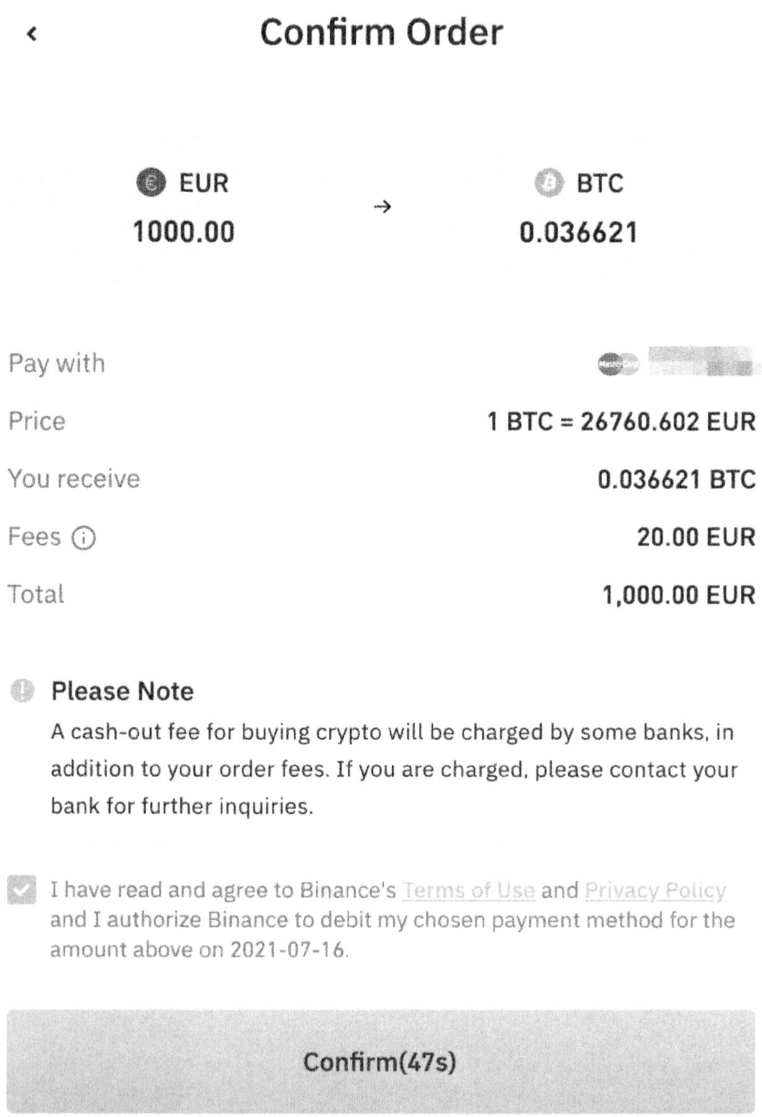

WHEN TO BUY AND SELL

When to Buy

In theory, it makes sense to buy investments while they are cheaper and then sell them when they reach their peak. This, however, is significantly more complicated than it appears. It's extremely tough to time the market, and it's much more difficult with cryptocurrencies because these assets are far more volatile than ordinary stock. If you buy now because prices appear to have reached a bottom, there's a chance they'll fall further, and you'll have bought too soon. However, if you wait too long, prices may increase, and you will have missed your chance.

The key is to buy strategically. Dollar-Cost Averaging (DCA) is one of the most effective strategies for doing so. When you regularly invest a set amount of money, such as $2,000 every quarter or $500 every month, you're doing dollar-cost averaging. Sometimes, you will buy at price peaks. You will, however, invest at other periods when prices are lower. The highs and lows should eventually level out. You won't have to worry about timing your purchases, and market volatility will have less of an influence on your assets.

As with most investments, the secret to making money in crypto is buying good investments and holding them for the long term. If they're truly good investments, they should appreciate in value over time, and their prices should rise in tandem. When you decide to invest, keep in mind that longevity is key. Nobody knows whether cryptocurrencies will succeed or not, but if they do, you may increase your profits by investing in the long run.

When to Sell

As we covered in Chapter Two, a successful exit strategy might be based on timing and price. Exits are when profits are achieved, while entrance points allow the opportunity to develop a portfolio. When a specific price objective is reached in the future, each investor should be judicious in withdrawing their principal as well as profits earned along the road. If the market enters a bear market (a period of falling prices), consider re-entering to profit from future gains.

STORING YOUR CRYPTOCURRENCIES

After you buy cryptocurrency, another crucial step is to figure out how to protect and safeguard it. Most newbies often choose to store their cryptocurrencies on the platform where they bought them. This is not a very smart idea as it is the equivalent of buying a car and leaving it in the dealer's ownership.

The most crucial thing to remember about cryptocurrency in making these decisions is that it is a custody asset. This means that if you acquire a coin on an exchange, you must withdraw it to a cryptocurrency wallet that you own. Otherwise, you will not be considered the owner. If you keep your coins on your exchange account, where they were put after purchase, they are still theoretically in the exchange's control. This means that if the exchange is hacked or goes out of business, your cryptocurrencies might just go with the exchange.

Thus, the smart move is to store your cryptocurrency in a wallet that you own and control.

Wallets

Cryptocurrency ownership differs from regular cash ownership in that you will never be able to hold a bitcoin in the palm of your hand. Cryptocurrency is a collection of codes rather than a tangible object. The blockchain stores cryptocurrency with a unique address, and other users can send you crypto using your public key while your crypto is unlocked with a private key.

In the same way that you use a standard wallet to keep your money safe, you can use a crypto wallet to do the same. Your cash, credit cards, IDs, and other valuables could all be stolen if someone gained access to your standard wallet. Fortunately, crypto wallets have additional security protections compared to traditional wallets. Crypto wallets contain the keys to your cryptocurrency rather than the coin itself. A wallet stores the information that allows you to connect to your money and keep it safe.

Wallets provide a safe place to keep digital valuables. Keeping your cryptocurrency in your personal wallet rather than on an exchange ensures that the private key to your funds is only accessible to you. It also enables you to store funds outside of an exchange, lowering the risk of your assets being stolen in the event your exchange is hacked.

Types of Wallets

You have a number of alternatives when it comes to selecting a crypto wallet. The concept of hot wallets (online wallets) and cold wallets is the first thing you should consider.

Hot Wallets: Hot wallets are online wallets. They run on devices such as computers, phones, and tablets. These internet-connected gadgets generate the private keys to your currencies, posing a risk from increased accessibility. While a hot wallet allows you to access and transfer funds fast, putting your private key on an internet-connected device makes it more vulnerable to hacking.

Money can be stolen if these hot wallets are used without sufficient security. This happens frequently and in various ways. For instance, it would be foolish to brag about your bitcoin holdings in a public place like Reddit while utilizing minimal security and storing them in a hot wallet. However, with proper measures, these wallets can be made secure. Strong passwords, two-factor authentication, and secure internet browsing should be standard.

For modest sums of cryptocurrencies or cryptocurrency actively traded on exchanges, think of a hot wallet as a checking account. Conventional financial advice says to only spend money in a checking account and save or invest the rest. Hot wallets are in the same boat.

Cold Wallets: A cold wallet is not linked to the internet and is less likely to be compromised. These wallets are also known as offline or hardware wallets. Some of these wallets have software that works in parallel with the user's private key so they can view their portfolio without risking their private key.

Paper Wallets: A paper wallet is the most secure way to keep cryptocurrency offline. A paper wallet is a wallet that may be generated from an online platform. It then prints out both public and private keys on paper. You can only access the cryptocurrency in these addresses if you have the private key on paper. Many people laminate these paper wallets and keep them in bank safe deposit boxes or even in their home safe. Because you can't sell or trade bitcoin kept in these wallets, they're designed for long-term investments.

Hardware Wallet: A hardware wallet is a USB drive that securely contains a user's private keys. Unlike hot wallets, these wallets are unaffected by infections on the computer. The private keys never touch a networked computer or software. These gadgets are often open-source, allowing the community to assess their safety rather than a corporation doing so.

A good wallet setup includes:

- An exchange account for buying and selling.
- A hot wallet for holding small to medium quantities of crypto.
- A cold hardware wallet for long-term holdings.

KEEPING YOUR WALLET SAFE

Use a Secure Internet Connection

When trading or doing crypto transactions, use only a secure internet connection and avoid public Wi-Fi networks. For increased security, use a VPN even when connected to your home network. A VPN masks your IP address and location, keeping your online activities safe and private from malicious attackers.

Manage Multiple Wallets

You can diversify your bitcoin investments by using numerous wallets because there are no restrictions on wallet creation. Use one wallet for daily transactions and another for everything else. This will protect your cryptocurrency assets and lower the chances of a security breach.

Keeping Your Personal Device Safe

To protect against newly identified vulnerabilities, make sure your personal device is up to date with the newest virus definitions. Use a powerful antivirus and firewall to boost your device's security and prevent hackers from exploiting the issue by writing apps to target the vulnerability.

Change Your Passwords Regularly

When it comes to security, the value of a strong password cannot be overstated. Make sure you have a strong, complicated, and difficult-to-guess password that you change regularly. If you have multiple wallets, ensure you have multiple passwords for each wallet. For added protection, use two-factor authentication (2FA) or multi-factor authentication (MFA).

DIVERSIFICATION

If you follow the basic rules of long-term investing—rebalancing regularly, so you have a diversified portfolio—you're probably familiar with the idea that you don't want to invest too heavily in one asset or security. But "diversifying" a crypto portfolio is much different from diversifying a portfolio of stocks and bonds. Here's how it can help.

In traditional investing, diversification is a hedge against the poor performance of one asset class. Investors usually diversify into secondary non-related asset classes that could survive or even thrive when their primary asset classes crash. This diversification benefit doesn't apply very much in crypto, as cryptocurrencies generally move in tandem.

So, in crypto, diversification is a hedge against total loss for those instances where a coin goes to zero. If one cryptocurrency fails and your investment goes all the way to zero, other crypto investments may still do well. Ideally, your whole crypto portfolio won't be wiped out because of one coin.

Of course, diversifying could potentially limit your winnings. But, look at it this way. Owning ten coins instead of one improves your odds of getting a ride to the moon, even if, perhaps, it eliminates your chance of getting a ride to Pluto.

How to Diversify Your Crypto Portfolio

Diversify By Industry

Make sure you invest in a diverse set of coins that can be used to tackle issues in various industries. This will help mitigate the adverse effects of crypto-unfriendly policies and events on your investment. Make sure that you do thorough research and invest in both solid and fast-growing businesses. You should also evaluate overall profitability and globally competitive industries, such as medicine and finance.

Diversify By Geography

Ensure that none of your funds are going to crypto projects in the same region or country—conduct thorough research on the performance of crypto projects in different parts of the world. Doing so will shield your investments from regulatory uncertainty and provide you with an additional means of balancing out your diverse portfolio even in uncertain market conditions.

Diversify By Timing

Although it is impossible to eliminate market risk when investing entirely, you can increase the value of your portfolio by being careful about when and where you invest. An interval-based investment strategy is to diversify your investments by timing, also known as dollar-cost averaging. Many exchanges allow you to set automated purchasing to make regular investments automatically.

BITCOIN VS. TRADITIONAL INVESTMENTS

Crypto vs. Stocks

Both cryptocurrencies and equities have ups and downs. Stocks are subject to corporate and financial risks, market volatility, and government regulations. However, cryptocurrencies are decentralized. A government or a group does not control them. Crypto has outperformed stocks in the short period it has existed. However, stocks have a long history, making future predictions easier.

Crypto vs. Bonds

Bonds are an individual's loan to a firm or the state. In other words, when an investor buys bonds, the corporation or government that sold them owes them money. After some time, the corporation or the government will pay back the entire sum. Bonds are highly secure, especially government bonds. The main drawback of bonds is that returns are poor as interests are low.

Bitcoin vs. Precious Metals

Gold and other precious metals are far more stable than crypto. Investing in precious metals carries concerns such as mobility, import fees, and, most importantly, security. Cryptocurrencies, on the other hand, do not require physical transfer. Because it's all digital, it's easy for the investor to hold.

12 THINGS TO KNOW BEFORE YOU GO INTO CRYPTOCURRENCY

1. Bitcoin can be bought with fiat currency.

This is an essential fact that crypto newbies often do not know. You can buy virtual currencies with a debit, credit, or bank card. Coinbase and Binance are two beginner-friendly cryptocurrency exchanges. Other more popular platforms like Paypal also offer the ability to buy crypto using regular currency.

2. Be mindful of FOMO (fear of missing out).

Popular cryptocurrencies' prices may rise drastically and quickly in a bull market. Proceed with caution: purchasing BTC at exorbitant prices could result in huge losses if the market corrects.

3. Make a plan.

We have discussed the need for a plan; successful crypto investors create a strategy for their holdings. Setting a limit order, for example, can ensure that their Bitcoin is sold immediately whenever prices hit a certain level. On certain crypto exchanges, you may even duplicate the moves of established traders in the crypto market. CoinMarketCap and DataDash teamed up to create a cryptocurrency swing trading tutorial, which you can find here.

4. Choose a trustworthy crypto exchange.

Look for a crypto exchange with a lot of liquidity, a wide range of crypto assets, strong security measures, and credibility. The crypto information website CoinMarketCap has a page that rates exchanges based on how easy it is to buy bitcoin and provides more information about their regulation, and allowed payment methods for consumers who are buying Bitcoin for the first time. You can find it right here!

5. Never invest more than you can afford to lose.

Cryptocurrency is a riskier investment than a lot of other things. Nothing is guaranteed except volatility. Furthermore, it is uncontrollable in the vast majority of cases. This item does not have FDIC insurance or a buyer of last resort. The value of cryptocurrencies varies dramatically from minute to minute. As a result, don't risk your entire farm or life savings on a single penny.

6. Keep your private keys in a secure location.

Always keep in mind that your crypto must be protected. Earlier in the chapter, we discussed wallets and how to protect your crypto. No matter what choice of wallet you choose, the key is to always keep in mind that once lost, crypto is irretrievable.

7. Do your own research (DYOR).

Before investing a significant sum of money in any cryptocurrency, spend hours researching the technology to understand the value proposition and the risks. ("I'll sell it for a higher price to someone else") is not a value proposition.

Read as much as you can on the subject. Delve into developer mailing lists and community forums. It is recommended that you listen to podcasts. Borrow books from the library regarding digital currency and related fields, including cryptography, game theory, and economics. Go back and do some more study after you think you have learned everything there is to know. You're almost certainly not done yet.

8. Not your keys, not your crypto.

Like cash or jewelry, cryptocurrency is a bearer asset, meaning that the possessor is assumed to be the rightful owner. It's no longer there once it's misplaced or stolen. Advanced users will advise against entrusting the cryptographic keys of your crypto wallet to a third party, such as an exchange. In many cases, crypto exchanges are unregulated in many jurisdictions and may be vulnerable to hackers or exit scams (in which clients' money is stolen).

Aside from exploits, exchanges may block you from withdrawing your assets at any time for a variety of reasons ranging from bankruptcy to legal issues. Even so, some exchanges lack the infrastructure required to be open at all times. For example, Coinbase and Robinhood sometimes encounter downtime during periods of market volatility. If you don't have your own wallet, you can't be confident you have complete control over your coins.

9. You can buy a fraction of a bitcoin (and most other cryptos).

You are not required to purchase the entire coin. Bitcoin, for instance, is divisible to the eighth decimal place. So, if you're curious about how Bitcoin works, you can pick one up for as low as $10 and try it out.

10. Consider the tax implications.

This is incredibly important for a variety of reasons. To begin with, the Internal Revenue Service (IRS) considers crypto assets to be property rather than currency when it comes to taxation. As a result, if you buy a coin for $1 and it doubles in value, you must record and pay tax on that capital gain, even if you spend the extra dollar on something as insignificant as a bag of chewing gum. Despite the lobbying efforts of the crypto business, there is no "de minimis exception." As always, before making any tax decisions consult your tax professional in your local area.

Furthermore, centralized exchanges provide account data to the IRS regularly. Cryptocurrency isn't regulated as strictly as stocks or banks. On the other hand, the federal government is in debt and will not hesitate to send in someone wearing mirrored aviator glasses to inquire about your cryptocurrency transactions.

11. Don't be concerned about prices; instead, make your purchases using dollar-cost averaging.

Markets fluctuate from day to day, hour to hour, and minute to minute, but any cryptocurrency or investment worth its salt is a long-term bet. The best strategy is to invest without being fixated on entry prices. With Dollar-Cost Averaging (discussed in Chapter Four), you can make steady investments without being bogged down by prices.

12. Be on the lookout for scammers.

You may have heard a lot of talk on social media about a new investment strategy that promises enormous returns from obscure crypto assets. Others make exaggerated predictions about the price of Bitcoin's rise. Unfortunately, some people in the cryptocurrency sector are dishonest, and Ponzi schemes and exit scams have cost billions of dollars.

Scammers rely on their victims developing a sensation of FOMO, or fear of missing out. Before investing in cryptocurrencies, think about your alternatives carefully, and remember that if something seems too good to be true, it probably is. There are numerous neutral reviews and fiercely independent news sources in the bitcoin industry that can help you make an informed decision.

5

BEWARE OF THE RISKS

Reality and Cryptocurrency Risks

Investing in cryptocurrency carries a high level of risk. The risks connected with cryptocurrencies vary depending on who is involved in the trading cycle: financial institutions, non-financial organizations, and individual investors. These dangers can range from typical crypto price volatility to targeted schemes.

Scalability

Despite the enormous growth in the number of currencies and the number of people wanting to adopt crypto, the number of transactions is still small compared to credit and cash transactions. The big question is whether cryptocurrency can transition from a "shiny new thing" into widespread usage and utility.

Some individuals and businesses believe that one or more cryptocurrencies will eventually replace national currency in transactions. However, one major impediment to cryptocurrencies replacing national currencies is that they are usually more expensive to transact with than most national currencies (taking together the costs borne by both parties to the transaction). As a result, most private parties have little motivation to use bitcoins.

If the cost of cryptocurrency transactions does not fall significantly, claims that cryptocurrencies will eventually replace national currency will lose credibility, and this source of value will become significantly less.

Volatility Risk

The risk of unanticipated market movements is referred to as volatility risk. Sometimes, volatility might be advantageous because it's difficult to make money in a market that is not changing, but it can also catch you off guard. Like any other market, the bitcoin market may go the opposite direction of your predictions. You risk losing your investment if you are not prepared for market volatility. Cryptocurrencies have no intrinsic value, and as a result, their value could plummet at any time.

Security Risk

Have you ever heard of cryptocurrency scams, hackings, or cyber theft? These have been a hot topic in the cryptocurrency sector since Bitcoin's inception in 2009. With each scandal, the value of cryptocurrencies suffers a temporary setback. As a result, safety precautions must be taken at every level of your bitcoin investment strategy. We'll go over the many types of fraud you can encounter while investing in crypto later in this chapter.

Absence of Regulations

Many people argue that the lack of a regulatory framework makes bitcoin investments increasingly risky. If the technology is mastered and the problems are overcome, cryptocurrency might be a terrific investment. Even yet, the investment platform will remain risky without government oversight. There are certain other risks as well, of a logistical nature.

In many jurisdictions, ownership of cryptocurrencies is not enforceable in court. Thus if a coin is stolen or lost, an investor has no remedy to retrieve it. Similarly, if deals are executed on terms that differ from those agreed to, an investor usually has little legal recourse.

Furthermore, the tax position of cryptocurrencies may change in the future, and it varies per country. It is still unclear if it is money or a commodity in many nations due to a lack of effective laws. While profits from cryptocurrency investments are frequently subject to capital gains tax, reporting procedures are frequently ambiguous. It is critical that you thoroughly examine your country's situation to avoid having your winnings revoked due to vague legislation.

Liquidity Risk

The risk of not being able to sell (or liquidate) an investment quickly and at a reasonable price is known as liquidity risk. Cryptocurrencies are not immune to illiquidity. Price manipulation is a possibility when liquidity is scarce. One significant participant can immediately shift the market in their favor by placing a large order. On the plus side, as bitcoin investment becomes more accessible and acceptable, the market may become more liquid. Because the number of trustworthy crypto exchanges has grown, more people will be able to trade. Bitcoin users have gradually increased over the last decade. Thus the signs appear to be pointing toward continued growth.

Vanishing Risk

Hundreds of different cryptocurrencies are currently accessible. More and more cryptocurrencies are introduced every day. Many of these cryptocurrencies may become obsolete in the next ten years, while others may prosper. Consider the dot-com bubble as an example of a rapidly dissipating threat. Many people all around the world created businesses as the internet grew in popularity in the late 1990s. Some, such as Amazon and eBay, have conquered the globe. Many more perished in flames. It is likely that many of the blossoming cryptocurrencies springing up left and right are going to fail.

Will Bitcoin Crash Someday?

Two Yale University economists (Yukun Liu and Aleh Tsyvinski) produced research titled "Risks and Returns of Cryptocurrency" in 2018. They looked at the possibility of Bitcoin crashing to zero in a single day. The authors discovered that the likelihood of an undefined tragedy crashing Bitcoin to zero ranged from 0 to 1.3 percent and was around 0.4 percent at the time of publishing, using Bitcoin's history returns to determine its risk-neutral disaster probability. For some context, in an interview with YaleNews, Tsyvinski indicated that the euro (EUR) had a 0.009% probability of doing the same.

Others claim that Bitcoin will inevitably crash to zero because Bitcoin has no intrinsic value. On the other hand, Bitcoin advocates argue that the currency is backed by customer confidence and mathematics. Despite the fact that Bitcoin is frequently pitted against government currencies, both Bitcoin and "fiat" currencies such as the US dollar (USD) and the Pound sterling (GBP), which were previously backed by gold (which has intrinsic value), currently have no physical backing. Of course, some would argue that at least the US dollar is backed by debt.

One of the most common arguments for Bitcoin's eventual demise is a sophisticated con. Bitcoin skeptics say Bitcoin's development is overseen by a central committee of developers, which solely favors the powerful. Another prominent argument advanced by Sharma and other critics, including Warren Buffet and Mark Cuban, is that Bitcoin is simply overvalued due to its lack of utility. However, it might be argued that the benefit of Bitcoin is directly proportional to the number of users. This has been observed with the introduction of new cryptocurrency use cases. Cryptocurrency was initially used for peer-to-peer barter before internet trading became a thing, and now there's an entire ecosystem of DeFi products that expand its utility even further.

If Bitcoin genuinely crashed to zero, it would either indicate that trading or exchanging it for goods and services became impossible or that buy-side liquidity plummeted to zero for some cause. One of the few probable possibilities that may lead to this is if Bitcoin is outlawed by all world governments, making it illegal to own or use, as it is in a few nations currently.

This would also necessitate shutting down the whole Bitcoin network, rendering all nodes—including those in space—inaccessible and making it impossible to create new ones. Theoretically, this would make Bitcoin transmission difficult and prevent underground transactions, rendering the currency useless.

This situation, however, would be nearly impossible to achieve. The Bitcoin blockchain's entire value proposition is decentralization by the worldwide distribution of network nodes. While opinions on the value of Bitcoin fluctuate, almost everyone agrees that Blockchain is a game-changing technology. This means that as long as the Blockchain remains decentralized, it will be nearly impossible to bring it down alongside Bitcoin.

Another possibility is that Bitcoin will be rendered obsolete by a superior cryptocurrency or a similar alternative payment mechanism (and therefore worthless as a payment method or store of value). However, this scenario would most certainly take several years, if not decades, to play out.

Given all of this, it's possible Bitcoin may crash. However, this does not appear to be very likely.

Sustainability of Cryptocurrency

Cryptocurrencies are becoming increasingly popular as a means of payment. Considering everything that requires electricity in the traditional banking system, such as data centers, ATMs, corporate offices, transportation, and so on, cryptocurrencies use less than 40% of conventional banking's electricity.

However, cryptocurrencies are still powered mainly by fossil fuels, and Bitcoin mining consumes more energy than the Philippines in a year. Elon Musk said in May 2021 that Tesla would no longer accept bitcoin for vehicle purchases owing to concerns about the "rapidly expanding consumption of fossil fuels for bitcoin mining." He referenced data from Cambridge University researchers that suggests bitcoin's electricity usage has increased this year.

Cryptocurrencies are created and circulated through mining. This procedure necessitates the use of advanced computers to tackle extremely difficult computational arithmetic problems. This mining process also necessitates a great deal of upkeep. Because bitcoin is a decentralized system, it is vital to establish a mechanism that allows miners to audit all transactions. As a result, a tremendous amount of electricity is required.

For crypto mining, a sustainable alternative could be to use renewable energy. This could be a way to drive the adoption of sustainable energy sources. Cryptocurrency exchanges that locate mining facilities near renewable energy farms can make use of excess electricity that would otherwise be wasted. In an attempt to make bitcoin mining more environmentally friendly, Cambridge's Global Cryptoasset Benchmarking Study in 2018 found that 39 percent of mining was fueled by hydroelectric energy. Nonetheless, like those in China and Canada, many Bitcoin miners employ low-cost hydropower for a while before switching back to fossil fuels.

The crypto industry is already responding to sustainability challenges. New coins and technologies are creating better systems that require less energy. The likely replacement to "proof of work" is the "proof of stake" system. Proof of stake is more sustainable because it attributes mining power to a miner's fraction of coins owned rather than the number of computations. Cryptocurrencies employing proof of work might reduce their energy use by 99.99 percent by modifying their mining method. Ethereum is currently working on their 2.0 update which will use proof-of-stake among other improvements. This is planned to be released in 2022.

Whether or not crypto is the future, it is critical to continue to assess the impact of cryptocurrencies on the environment and improve their long-term viability.

Identifying and Avoiding Scams

Transparency and verified trust are the cornerstones of cryptocurrency. Unfortunately, the sector has been plagued by a slew of bad-faith actors attempting to defraud users of their hard-earned coins and investments by exploiting the industry's expansion.

Here are some popular scam schemes, as well as how to spot and avoid them.

Imposter Websites

Even if you are following a good suggestion from someone with a lot of experience, you can still become a victim by accessing a bogus website by accident. A surprising amount of websites have been created to look like legitimate startup companies. Think twice if the URL bar doesn't have a small lock icon indicating security and the site address doesn't begin with "HTTPS."

Even though the site appears to be the same as the one you thought you were visiting, you may be sent to a different payment platform.

For instance, suppose you click on a link that appears to be from a real website, but the attackers have crafted a phony URL with a zero instead of an 'o'. Of course, that platform isn't going to the bitcoin investment you've already looked at. To avoid this, make sure you write the URL exactly as it appears in your browser. Also, double-check it.

Fake Apps for Mobile Devices

Scammers also use bogus apps accessible for download on Google Play and the Apple App Store to deceive cryptocurrency investors. Although stakeholders can immediately identify and delete bogus apps, this doesn't imply that the apps aren't influencing many businesses. According to Bitcoin News, tens of thousands of individuals have already downloaded fraudulent bitcoin apps.

While Android users are at a higher risk, every investor should be aware of the possibilities. Are there any glaring misspellings in the copy, including the app's name? Is there an inauthentic look to the branding, such as odd color or an erroneous logo? Take note of this and think twice before downloading.

Fraudulent Tweets and Other Social Media Posts

We all know things may not be what they seem when it comes to social media. You can't be sure you're not following impostor accounts if you follow celebrities and CEOs on social media. The same is true in cryptocurrency, where malicious, impersonating bots abound. Don't believe offers from Twitter or Facebook, especially if the outcome appears to be unattainable. Fake accounts can be found all over the internet.

If you provide someone on these networks even a modest bit of your cryptocurrency, you're unlikely to get it back. Don't assume that they aren't bots just because others are responding to the offer. You must exercise extreme caution.

Email Scamming

Even if it appears to be an email from a respectable cryptocurrency organization, proceed with caution before investing your digital money. Is the email exactly the same and the logo and branding? Are you able to confirm that the email address belongs to the company? One of the reasons it's crucial to choose a company with real people working for it is the opportunity to check on this. Ask someone who works there if you have any doubts about an email. Also, never go to a website by clicking on a link in an email.

Scammers frequently launch fraudulent ICOs (initial coin offerings) to steal large sums of money. Don't be fooled by these phony email or website offers. Take your time to examine every aspect. You must be certain of the legitimacy of any involved third-party services and merchants before sending cryptocurrency to a blockchain address. Only send cryptocurrency to businesses you trust.

Scams Involving Technical Support and Impersonation

Scam phone numbers are widely disseminated on the internet, tempting naive victims looking for help. Scammers may also make outbound calls to potential victims. These con artists are experts at social engineering, deceiving and manipulating their victims into supplying personal information that can be utilized for fraudulent purposes by making false claims.

Never grant remote access to your device to support employees (or anybody else for that matter). The scammer now has complete control over your computer, online financial accounts, and digital existence. Never give out your security codes or passwords for 2FA (2-Factor Authentication). When it comes to your crypto platforms and wallets, outbound calls requesting confidential personal information should never be accepted.

Giveaway Scams

Scammers are making use of social media to spread their giveaway schemes. They upload screenshots of fabricated company and management correspondence promoting a giveaway with links to bogus websites. Fake accounts will then reply to these posts, confirming the legitimacy of the hoax. After that, the fake websites will ask you to "verify" your address by transferring cryptocurrency to the scam giveaway.

Under the pretense of address verification, never send cryptocurrency to giveaways. All giveaways and offers found on social media should be taken with a grain of salt. Screenshots in reply messages should not be trusted since they might be falsified and manipulated. Do some research on any entity courting you on social media using your favorite search engine. Remember that if an offer appears too good to be true, it most likely is.

Scams of Extortion

Scammers frequently leverage data from other websites' data breaches to deceive you into believing they have more information on you than they actually do. They might, for example, offer you an old password that you used to confirm that their scam is real.

If you are a victim of an extortion scheme, please take the following steps right away:

- Report the email to your email provider as spam.
- Use a trustworthy malware scanner to perform a preventive malware scan on your computer.
- If you recognize any of the passwords supplied in the extortion email as ones you presently use on other websites, change them immediately.
- Make a police report with your local authorities.

These messages can be frightening, but they are almost always false.

Multi-Level-Marketing Scams

To sell their coins and tokens, multi-level marketing crypto companies use a layered recruitment and commission system. While some MLMs are legitimate, the vast majority of those in the crypto field are Ponzi schemes. MLMs come in various shapes and sizes, but they always have something in common, emphasizing recruitment instead of sales and providing a financial return based on new recruit payments. proMany members are motivated primarily by the possibility to earn money by recruiting others.

You're told to buy the ABC Token, and you will automatically join their MLM program, and that for every person you recruit or bring in who purchases a token, a piece of their payment will go into your wallet.

HOW TO MANAGE RISKS

It's vital to remember that crypto trading isn't only about making money; it's also about taking risks and avoiding losses. And, if you don't want to lose your entire deposit on the first day, you must follow risk management guidelines. The appropriate method can help you make a lot of money while lowering your risk of losing money.

Risk management is the ability to anticipate and mitigate potential losses from a failed transaction. For example, you chose to invest in cryptocurrencies and spent your entire deposit only on Binance Coin (BNB), a relatively powerful and steady project. The market, however, fluctuates, and prices can drop by as much as 50%.

A single deal can cause you to lose half of your deposit. This is, of course, a highly dramatic case. We are confident that you, our reader, will avoid such blatant errors. But the simple fact is that if you don't have a risk management strategy in place and trade intuitively, you will almost certainly lose money.

How to Avoid Losing Money and Trade Safely

Do Your Research

Before investing in any cryptocurrency, make sure you do your homework and invest within your means. It's not a good idea to invest just because you're feeling left out or without consulting an investing expert. It is also important to understand that no matter the research and analysis you have done, or the assurances from expert traders, the market can always go in the opposite direction. This is why you have to make sure that you invest what you can afford to lose.

Understand Your Reward-to-Risk Ratio

The reward-to-risk ratio is the amount of money you can make for every unit of currency you risk. Invest only as much as you are willing to lose. Keep in mind that not every trade will be profitable. Even the most experienced traders lose money. Losing is unavoidable in trading; you must accept it. The profit/loss ratio is the most crucial factor to consider. It should ideally be 3 to 1 or at least 2 to 1.

Diversify Your Portfolio

Investing in a number of different crypto coins can assist in reducing risk. A diverse portfolio minimizes the amount of risk in the portfolio. The impact of volatility can be mitigated when investments are made across multiple coins. Some cryptocurrencies have a lot of volatility, whereas others don't. You could lose half your money if you put your entire deposit into one cryptocurrency, and it suddenly drops by 50%. However, if you have ten assets and Ripple was just 10% of your total stake, your loss will be much smaller. As a result, risk diversification should never be overlooked! Always keep an eye on the market and diversify your cryptocurrency investments.

Establish Your Entry and Exit Strategies

Your transactions would not be complete without your entry and exits. A solid entry is a cherry on top of a winning trade. However, you must weigh both gains and losses when it comes to exits. A strong risk management strategy requires you to plan your escape points. Remember our discussion on planning. You must have your strategy in place and not let the market decide when to enter or exit.

RISK VS. REWARDS

When it comes to investing, determining your individual risk tolerance is crucial. Many investors use the risk-to-reward ratio to compare predicted investment returns. In general, the bigger the danger, the larger the profit. Conversely, the smaller the risk, the lower the gain.

When someone makes a low-risk investment, they are less likely to lose money, but they are also less likely to benefit from aggressive growth as part of their investment strategy. If you only invest in low-risk investments, it may take a long time for you to make a significant profit.

On the other hand, high-risk investments can reward risk-takers handsomely and fast. Assuming greater risk is connected with a higher projected return. Your investing risk tolerance, financial needs, and timescale are all factors to consider. As individuals, investors should never invest more than they can afford to lose, especially when it comes to risky investment profiles.

Compared to more typical investment instruments, crypto investing carries a significant level of risk. Some crypto coins, such as Bitcoin and Ether, have a higher level of security than others. It's critical to understand the risks and technical and fundamentals associated with the assets, as well as any correlations to other asset classes, as with any asset class. When it comes to crypto investing, the risk vs. reward decision is between losing your investment due to price volatility vs.

taking advantage of the significant rewards presented by the new crypto opportunity. Early investors that believe in the cryptocurrency market's long-term potential are betting that it will continue to rise. If this turns out to be true (as most people believe), the benefits will almost certainly outweigh the hazards.

Diversification is the answer once again in this case. To achieve your financial objectives, you must build a varied portfolio. Diversification can help you lower your risk and increase your profit chances. Bitcoin is a new asset that investors should consider in their portfolios as part of their overall diversification plan. Even though it is now one of the riskier investments, many people believe it has a lot of room to develop and only accounts for a small portion of other financial assets.

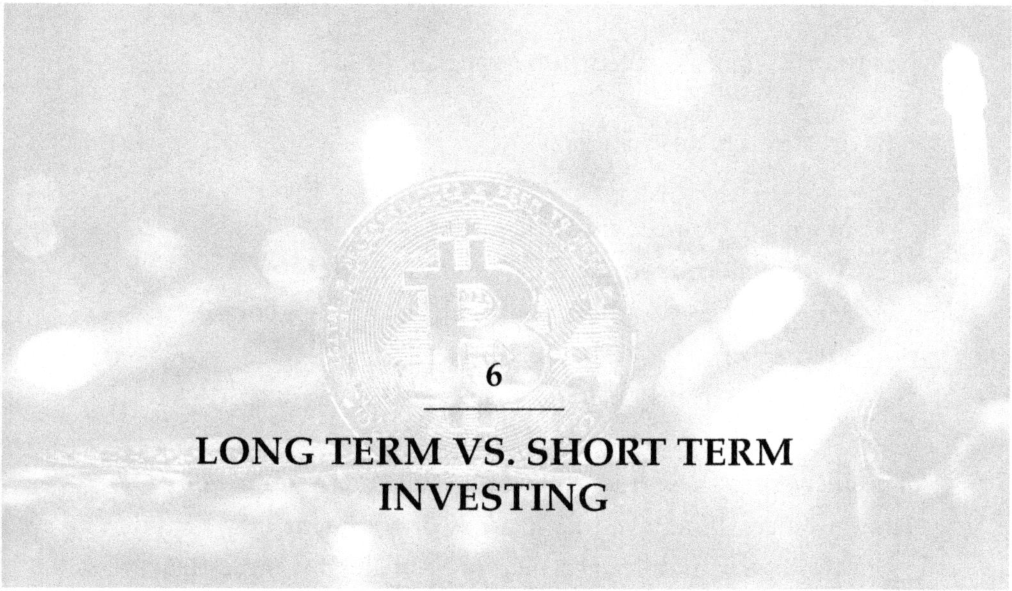

6

LONG TERM VS. SHORT TERM INVESTING

Whether in the stock market, real estate, or cryptocurrency, the primary purpose of investment is for financial returns. It is always important to remember this, especially with crypto, where people may get carried away and lose money while "enjoying the ride." The length of time in which these returns are expected determines the nature of the investment. This is categorized into short-term and long-term investing.

Now, there are no fixed terms, but we can generally say that short-term investments can be anything from a day to a year long. Long-term investments are from a year upward. With cryptocurrencies, the decision as to whether you are in for the long term or the short term is critical because the decision will determine the type of coins you invested in and the type of trades and investments you'll be involved in.

Which is Better?

The advice on the term and length of an investment is not one-size-fits-all. The decision rests squarely on what your investment goals are.

The questions to answer are:

1. What do you need this return for?
2. When will you require these funds, if at all?
3. How long do you think you will be able to hold out if markets drop?
4. What is your risk tolerance level?

The answers to these questions can usually be found in your present circumstances. The investment needs of a student may be different from those of a middle-aged man or woman. But more than where you are, it depends on your goals.

For instance, if you want a nest egg for when your child grows up, then you clearly are in for a long-term investment. On the other hand, if you want to pay for college fees next session, you are clearly up for a short-term investment. The student can also invest with hopes of using the returns to start a business down the line after school, a long-term investment.

So, the question of which is better depends on the answers you come up with. We will further discuss the two investment terms and their benefits and risks to enable you to compare them and place them side by side with your investment goals to reach an informed decision.

SHORT-TERM PLANS FOR CRYPTOCURRENCY

Short-term investing refers to when a trader hangs on to their coins for less than a year and buys and sells more frequently. If you are a short-term investor, you are known as an "active trader." This is especially true if your goal is to make a large sum of money in a short period. Short-term investments can last anywhere from a few hours to several days or even weeks. This has a higher risk profile than long-term investing. However, in investing (and with many other things in life), the bigger the risk, the more likely the rewards. With crypto, this is perhaps even more true when it comes to short-term investments.

It's worth noting that the shorter the time limit, the higher the danger of trading because the cryptocurrency market is unstable. For this reason, short-term investing is also referred to as "aggressive" trading. In other words, you are investing aggressively in the hopes of faster and better returns. It is also aggressive because there's a chance you will lose your money, and you are willing to take more significant risks and accept the possibility of losing your money.

Depending on the defined schedule, a lot can happen in the digital asset market. As a result, durations play an essential part in deciding the outcome of a trader's approach. With that in mind, here are some of the reasons why short-term investing can be more profitable than long-term investing

It Leverages Current Trends

The latest happenings in the crypto market strongly influence short-term investments. Users can watch the market and make informed trading selections based on what they learn. For example, in early 2021, Tesla founder Elon Musk announced that Tesla would be accepting Bitcoin payments (As we discussed earlier, Tesla did not go through with this due to Musk's sustainability concerns regarding Bitcoin's use of electricity). Such announcements can cause a spike in Bitcoin prices, meaning profit for a short-term investor.

Requires Less Capital

Long-term investors make large bets because they believe in the future of a crypto asset. On the other hand, cryptocurrency volatility does not guarantee that investors will save their money. In short-term investing, investors can make money with a modest quantity of money. It alleviates the burden of needing more cash to accumulate earnings. Short-term traders can increase their money as time goes on, based on their budgets.

The Market is Active

The bitcoin market is dynamic and runs 24 hours a day, seven days a week. Because it is such a large and active market, short-term investors make aggressive trading selections to increase their profits. As a result, short-term crypto investments can be trusted by anyone at any moment.

Immediate Reinvestment

Investors that use short-term approaches can reinvest their profits right away. Long-term tactics like staking let investors keep track of their assets and, in most cases, keep them safe in digital wallets. As a result, users are restricted from reinvesting in their rising currencies. Short-term trading removes these limitations and allows investors to invest more after generating a profit.

Limits the Hassle of Researching

Any investing journey begins with learning more about a currency's offerings. On the other hand, short-term trading tactics take less study time than long-term trading strategies. Short-term traders need to comprehend the most fundamental facts to continue trading.

Because customers will commit their holdings for a more extended period, long-term strategies take a complete approach. Long-term investors may, in the end, lose money despite putting in the effort to investigate.

If you decide that short-term investing is the way to go, here are trading strategies to help you get started. Many of these strategies come from stock trading but apply just as well to crypto trading.

Day Investing

This is a method utilized by short-term traders, and it entails the trader watching the crypto market closely and actively to know and assess how to make his transaction. This is normally done with a great deal of dedication and commitment for the trader to keep track of market developments.

Day trading takes advantage of the volatility of crypto prices. The investor puts in money and takes it out quickly by the end of the day, hopefully at higher prices. In this technique, the trader seeks to make frequent though usually small profits to build up a significant sum. Day trading is extremely risky with no certainty of profit. We advise only experts to day trade crypto assets. As a beginner, it is advisable to begin investing in more stable cryptos over the longer term. This is lower risk and requires less time allocated to research and analysis. One of the best ways to invest as a beginner, as described earlier, is dollar-cost averaging.

Despite this, day trading can be an excellent way to make money investing in crypto. If you are willing to sacrifice several hours a day and make informed and careful decisions, you can make regular and substantial profits on your investments, depending on how volatile the prices have been for the day.

Scalping

In this short-term trading technique, the trader buys and sells many times in a single day, resulting in multiple stock trades. Investors who trade penny stocks do so because they can buy and sell them very quickly, sometimes within minutes.

Any trader who wants to apply this bitcoin technique should have at least a no-commission brokerage account so that if they purchase and sell in minutes, they don't lose money. To increase their chances of success during scalping, traders should focus on one currency pair or position at a time.

As previously stated, the strategy can yield minor gains for each transaction while also posing a low risk. It's a helpful tool for new crypto traders who want to study and gain expertise. For a start, it is recommended that you invest a small amount of money. Scalping also uses a small amount of money and a smaller number of coins to keep track of as many changes as possible.

Swing Trading

Swing trading in the crypto market detects a price pattern that repeats itself and then profits from it by buying or selling the stock. This method is advisable if you have gained some experience in trading and investing, mainly if you can perform technical analysis and are well-versed in detecting and comprehending charts and indications. This technique relies heavily on the technical analysis of charts. To use this approach effectively, the user must also be familiar with peaks and declines, as well as other patterns.

LONG-TERM PLANS FOR CRYPTOCURRENCY

Long-term suggests that if you invest in cryptocurrency, you don't expect to see results right away, but rather over time. In cryptocurrency, long-term investing is a bet that the value and utility of cryptocurrency will keep increasing in the future and perhaps replace current monetary systems. This is a big bet which (as shown from the early investors in Bitcoin) can yield enormous returns.

The strategy for long-term investment is simple—choose the correct coins, buy and hold. The key ingredient in this form of investing is time, as no one can say for sure how it will play out. Only time will tell. As Warren Buffet puts it, "Some things simply require time."

However, if the past five years are anything to go by (Bitcoin has grown 7000% as of September 2021), you should take the bet. When it comes to long-term crypto investing, Bitcoin and Ethereum are the usual favorites. This choice is based on their value, publicity, and utility. Later in this chapter, we will discuss how to choose the right coins for long-term investing.

Long-term investing has numerous benefits, but here are the three major ones.

Less Risk

The biggest benefit of long-term investing is that the risk is reduced. While crypto prices are always volatile, coins such as Bitcoin have maintained steady growth in the past few years. With long-term investing, the volatility does not affect you as they come and go, and your prices remain in the long run.

In addition, When you constantly move in and out of the market, you risk missing out on a profitable opportunity while you are outside the market. With long-term investing, prices may rise and fall, and you will remain to reap the benefits.

It Works

It has worked in the past. Investing is a long-term endeavor. Some indices have similar rates of return over a five-year period. In this period, the S&P 500 has an average return of 60%, while the FTSE 100 has an average return of 25%. Markets tend to rise every five years. Therefore this happens almost every five years throughout history. The cryptocurrency market has grown by nearly 10,000% in the same period. Although such returns are unlikely to occur again in the foreseeable future, crypto may yet beat traditional investing markets if you give it time.

The Fees Are Lower

Transaction fees rise as a result of active trading. You will most likely incur less trading costs if you use the long-term plan, take the long-term view, and leave your investments alone after acquisition. A long-term investor does not trade daily. Therefore trading costs have little impact on their profits.

Long-Term Investment Strategy

Remember how we said in Chapter Two that the first step is to plan? Long-term investing necessitates a strategy; short-term investing necessitates moving with the market. Long-term is different because you're in it for the long haul and need a precise action plan for many eventualities.

Here are a few things to think about while investing for the long term:

- Will you sell when the cryptocurrency reaches a specific price or after a certain amount of time has passed?
- Will you sell your items in stages or all at once?
- Are you willing to give up your long-term goals in exchange for a quick profit?

For example, suppose investing conditions change or new laws are enacted that may impact your investment's economy and long-term prices. In that case, you should probably ponder selling before doing so.

To determine which cryptocurrencies are the most convenient or the finest to invest in for the long term, you must conduct extensive research.

How to Choose a Crypto Asset for the Long-Term

Cryptocurrencies can be evaluated for long-term worth in various ways, including market share, utility value, transaction volume, technology advancement, and market news. Here are some questions to ask about the cryptocurrency you're thinking about buying to see if it has long-term potential.

Market Share: What is the market share of this cryptocurrency in comparison to other currencies? A large market share indicates a dominant position. Make sure to compare the cryptocurrency project to similar competitors, as not all cryptocurrencies compete.

Utility Value: Is there a practical application for it? Do you think there's a market for users? What is the fundamental goal it aspires to achieve and is it viable to achieve that goal? Because it is a helpful and purposeful product, it is likely to be widely embraced and, as a result, is an excellent long-term investment.

Value of a Transaction: How frequently do people use cryptocurrency? Is it true that this sum has risen over time? A growing number of users suggests that a cryptocurrency is gaining traction and, as a result, is a good long-term investment.

Technology Development: Is there positive technological advancement appropriate for its intended purpose? Adapting technology to the objective increases the likelihood of adoption and, as a result, market share against competitors.

Market News: What is the current state of the market? Is there a problem that could have a long-term impact on your profitability? To make informed and healthy financial decisions, keep up with market news and trends.

SHORT-TERM RISKS

The biggest risk faced by short-term investors is that of the market's volatility. Volatility risk refers to the danger of unanticipated market changes. For instance, in March 2021, Bitcoin traded as high as $58,000. By April, it was $53,000, and by June, it fell to $30,000.

Volatility might be beneficial, but it can also sometimes take you off guard. Like any other market, the bitcoin market might go in the opposite direction of what you predict. If you are not prepared for market volatility, you risk losing your invested money.

LONG-TERM RISKS

As volatility might be the plague of short-term investing, long-term investing comes with its own set of dangers. For starters, we have no idea whether it will become a widely acknowledged money. If it doesn't, demand for it is likely to fall. Bitcoin's value will fall if demand decreases.

We also don't know what kind of regulatory challenges Bitcoin and other digital currencies might face. It's a dangerous proposition until more information emerges on that front. Even with all of this danger, Bitcoin may still be the best long-term investment there is.

EXCHANGING YOUR CRYPTO

Exchanging Your Crypto for a Better One

One of the fascinating aspects of cryptocurrency trading is that you can easily exchange one coin for another with ease. Due to the decentralized nature of cryptocurrency, no central authority or government sets the rules on what cryptocurrency you can or cannot have.

The implication is that, as a beginner, when you buy a coin and change your mind about the coin, you can exchange it for a better one. The choice of coins you can have or exchange is only limited by your funds and whether you can find an exchange that trades them.

There are various reasons you might want to exchange your coins. The most important one is that the coins you want are better than the ones you already have, especially for a particular purpose. For instance, you have been a short-term investor, putting your coins in more volatile coins to make faster returns. After some time, you decide to move to long-term investing. You can then exchange your Dogecoin to Bitcoin or Ethereum, which we have discussed may be more suited to long-term holding.

HOW TO EXCHANGE YOUR CRYPTOCURRENCY

As you may be aware, when you buy something or get a service, you are swapping money for the item or service you want. A "swap" usually means "exchanging one item or service of value for another (or many) items or service of worth (of similar value)," as the term implies.

In the same way, a "swap" in cryptocurrency refers to exchanging one cryptocurrency for the equivalent value of another. A swap is slightly different from an exchange.

With an exchange or a broker, you can pay for your cryptocurrency purchase with a "local" government-issued currency like USD or EUR when you buy it through a trade. In other cases, exchange platforms like Binance also allow you to swap one coin for another in specific trading pairs that they decide or pay for with the platform's token.

With a swap, however, there is no fiat cash involved. Instead, cryptocurrency is traded. During a swap, you pay with a cryptocurrency that isn't the same as the one you're going to buy. To swap your coin, you visit a swap platform and follow the steps. Some of the most popular swap platforms are Pancake Swap and Liquid.

PART III

GOING DEEPER

7

EXPANDING ON CRYPTOCURRENCY

CRYPTO TAXES

Before we go ahead, it is important to note that we do not provide tax, legal, or accounting advice. This book has been prepared for informational purposes only and is not intended to provide, and should not be relied on for, tax, legal, or accounting advice. You should consult your tax, legal, and accounting advisors before engaging in any transaction.

In the early days of cryptocurrency, rules and laws guiding the taxation of cryptocurrency were unclear and sometimes did not exist. Since then, a lot has changed with the growing popularity of cryptocurrencies, and the amount of money people have made. In light of this, tax regimes in countries across the world stepped up to formulate laws guiding the handling and taxation of crypto earnings and gains. For instance, in the US, the IRS stepped up crypto taxation in 2017 when bitcoin went mainstream.

By 2021, different countries will have different approaches to taxing crypto gains. Countries like Belarus, Germany, Portugal, Malta,

Hong Kong, El Salvador, and Malaysia treat crypto gains as tax-exempt. On the other hand, in the UK, crypto gains can be taxed as both income and capital gains, depending on the scenario. For instance, if you have put a significant amount of money, time, and effort into purchasing and trading cryptocurrency, you may be classified as a trader, and HMRC will tax your earnings. If HMRC considers you a trader, you'll need to register as a 'Sole Trader.' It's a good idea to consult a tax specialist to discover if you'll be classified as a trader by the IRS.

However, if you possess cryptocurrencies as an investment, you are treated as holding a foreign currency. As a result, you will be subject to capital gains tax. Only the amount of money you've acquired from the investment will be taxed, not the overall value of your bitcoin tax. In the UK, it's worth mentioning that if HMRC considers your cryptocurrency investment to be excessively speculative, you may not be taxed. Gambling profits and losses are also exempt from taxation. The most important thing is to keep track of all your deals and their worth.

The key to handling your crypto tax issues is to know what and how these rules apply to you. Therefore you mustn't ignore this and research your city, state, and country for the relevant laws. It is essential to understand that while the currencies might be virtual, the taxes are real.

With that in mind, let's discuss the tax requirements in the US.

What Are Crypto Taxes?

For federal income tax reasons, cryptocurrency is considered "property." The IRS recognizes it as a capital asset for the average investor. This means that crypto taxes are the same as taxes on any other capital gain earned on the sale or exchange of a capital asset.

You set a basis equal to the cost of acquisition when you buy a capital item, whether it's a stock, bond, property, widget, Bitcoin, or other investment. You calculate whether you made a profit or a loss when you sell anything by comparing the sales proceeds to the basis. You have a capital gain if your gains are higher than your basis. If the situation is reversed, you will suffer a capital loss.

You should also evaluate the length of time you kept the asset. Depending on how long you hold your bitcoin, your earnings or losses will be classified as "short-term" or "long-term." This distinction will also significantly impact the amount of crypto taxes you must pay. Taxation has to factor in your decision whether to be a short-term or long-term investor, as we discussed in the last chapter.

Capital Gains and Losses in the Short Term

A short-term capital gain or loss occurs when you buy and sell an asset within 365 days. Wages, salaries, commissions, and other forms of earned income are taxed at the same rates as short-term profits.

Gains and Losses On Long-Term Capital Assets

The difference between the sales price and your basis is long-term capital gain or loss if you buy an asset and sell it after a year. Because the rates are often lower, you'll pay less tax on a long-term gain than on a short-term gain. Long-term capital gains, at the time of this writing, are subject to three different tax rates: 0%, 15%, and 20%. In this case, your earnings determine how much you pay.

How to Keep Crypto Taxes to a Minimum

Now that you've learned a little more about crypto taxes, which are essentially capital gains taxes, you'll need a set of tactics to help you optimise your tax.

1. Wait for your short-term gains to turn into long-term gains before investing.

As previously stated, depending on how long you own bitcoin, different capital gains rates will apply. Hold your cryptocurrencies long enough to turn short-term gains into long-term gains if you want to reduce your tax burden. It won't be easy, but if you have the discipline and courage to hold on to your crypto for at least a year before selling, you'll possibly pay a lower tax rate on capital gains.

2. Offset your capital gains and capital losses.

Another way to reduce the amount of money crypto investors have to pay in taxes is to offset capital gains with capital losses. This works by deducting taxable gains on cryptocurrencies or other investments that have risen in value from losses on crypto-assets sold throughout the year.

However, you should be aware that this method has limitations. You must first offset losses of the same sort when you recognize investment losses. Short-term losses, for example, reduce your short-term gains first, whereas long-term losses reduce your long-term gains.

After that, you can utilize either type of net loss to offset the other type of capital gain. So, if you have any remaining long-term capital gains, you can apply them against any excess short-term losses.

If you still have one, you can utilize a net capital loss to reduce your regular income. However, you can only utilize up to $3,000 in capital loss to reduce your regular income in any one year if you use this technique. The remaining amount can be carried forward to the next year to offset future profits or be used to reduce your regular income by up to $3,000.

3. Use a self-directed individual retirement account to invest in cryptocurrency.

Investing in a tax-deferred or tax-free Self-Directed Individual Retirement Account is another way to reduce your crypto tax liability

(SDIRA). As a result, you have the option of paying taxes later, when your taxable income may be lower in retirement, or paying taxes now when you contribute to your Roth SDIRA if you expect to pay greater taxes in retirement.

4. Give assets to a relative.

Another approach to reduce your crypto tax payment, depending on your plans for utilizing your wealth, is to give your cryptocurrency to family members.

The IRS permits you to make tax-free gifts of up to $15,000 per person per year. In most cases, the recipient may have a low enough income to avoid paying taxes on the appreciated property sold. At the very least, you'll pay less in taxes than you would if you sold the bitcoin yourself. This technique fits right in with your overall estate planning goals and how you want to distribute your wealth. That makes it something you should talk to an estate planner about first to be sure it fits into your overall plan.

What Is Your Risk Tolerance?

In investing, risk tolerance refers to the amount of variation in investment returns that an investor is ready to accept. When it comes to investing in crypto, risk tolerance is crucial. You should be honest with yourself about your ability and desire to withstand large swings in the value of your investments; if you take on too much risk, you risk panicking and selling at the wrong time.

Younger people with broader time horizons can and are encouraged to take on more risk than older people with shorter time horizons. However, age should not be used to determine whether or not to move asset classes. Typically, the more money you have, the more risk you are likely to take. Risk tolerance is influenced by the amount of time you have to invest, your future earning potential, and the presence of other assets such as a home, pension, social security, or an inheritance. When you have other, more stable sources of funds, you can often take more risk with investable assets.

The first step in knowing which cryptocurrencies are best for you is determining your risk tolerance. Traditionally, equities, equity funds, and ETFs are frequently associated with higher risk tolerance, whereas bonds, bond funds, and ETFs are commonly associated with lower risk tolerance. As we have discussed, cryptocurrencies are riskier than all these.

Here are some risk profiles for you to consider.

Aggressive Risk Tolerance

Aggressive investors are usually well-versed in the market. Individuals and institutional investors with a thorough grasp of securities and their proclivities can buy highly volatile products like small-company stocks that can drop to zero or options contracts that can expire worthlessly. Aggressive investors aim for maximum profits with maximum risk while retaining a basis of risk-free securities.

Moderate Risk Tolerance

Moderate investors are willing to take some risk with their money, but they take a balanced approach with five to ten-year time horizons. Moderate investors frequently pursue a 50/50 structure, combining the more stable and established coins with more risky and volatile ones.

Conservative Risk Tolerance

In their investment portfolios, conservative investors are willing to accept little or no volatility. It is rare to see these people in crypto as the market is risky. Typical examples are retirees who have worked for decades to amass a nest egg are afraid to risk their capital. A cautious investor looks for vehicles that are both guaranteed and liquid.

To assess your risk tolerance, consider the following:

Make a List of Your Objectives

Identifying your financial objectives will assist you in determining how much time you have to build your money and, as a result, how much risk you can accept with the assets you select. You should consider what you're saving for when you plan to take some or all of the funds and how long you'll use the funds.

In most cases, the longer the time frame, the more risk you can take because your money will have more time to recover if the market falls dramatically. Assume you wish to use your investments to pay for a down payment on a property. If you don't plan to withdraw the assets within the next five years, you can feel comfortable taking on additional risks. You'll want to be more cautious with your money if you need the money sooner.

Remember that your objectives, and hence your risk tolerance, may be linked to your financial stability. If you have a steady salary, minimal (or no) high-interest debt, and some funds set aside for discretionary expenditures, you may be more willing to take on greater risk. If you don't have to worry about covering all your monthly needs, you won't be as concerned if your investments lose value because you're not reliant on that income.

Consider How Comfortable You Are With Guaranteed Outcomes Versus Chance Outcomes

Crypto investing does not offer guaranteed returns. There is a chance you will lose your money, and just the thought of this is enough to dissuade some investors. Indeed, people are disproportionately fearful of loss. Losing something makes us much more unhappy than acquiring the same thing. In other words, if we lost $1000 on an investment, we might be twice as disappointed as if we made $1000 on the same investment.

Consider risk tolerance in terms of your comfort level with a guaranteed outcome versus a chance one. Would you rather have $1,000 in your pocket right now or a 50% chance of winning $5,000? If you'd rather receive $1,000 right now, you may have a lower risk tolerance due to your need for a definite outcome while missing out on the possibility of winning a larger prize.

If you picked the possibility to win $5,000, on the other hand, you might have a higher risk tolerance because you were willing to take the danger of losing everything for the chance to win more.

Consider Your Personal Level of Risk Tolerance

Of course, you'll want to think about how taking on riskier investments may affect your emotional state. Do you get stressed out when you check the price charts and see numbers in the red? Does negative market news easily throw you off? Would you be tempted to sell the asset much sooner than planned if you suffered losses? When determining whether or not to make a riskier investment, keep these reactions in mind.

Your risk tolerance has a significant influence on how you invest your money. Everyone's risk tolerance is different, but thinking about your objectives, comfort level with a possible outcome, and how market swings affect you emotionally can help you determine how much risk you can take.

When the Going Gets Tough

What to do/not to do when the marketplace seems "red."

When investing in cryptocurrency, it is almost certain that there will be days when the markets will swing against you. Experienced traders and investors have come to expect this and often take it in stride. For new investors, it can be quite shocking.

Here are some things to do when the market is red.

1. Maintain Your Composure

You must respond calmly whether you decide to sell your cryptocurrencies or consider a dip as an opportunity to buy more. Making emotional decisions, particularly while trading, rarely yields positive results. So, before rushing into the market in a frenzy, think about why you're trading cryptocurrency in the first place.

Traditional market investing, according to stockbrokers, requires a high level of mental discipline. They utilize that discipline to keep themselves in check when the market is volatile. This is how they stay on track with their approach and avoid making foolish decisions during tough times. With the high volatility of cryptocurrency, this mental discipline is even more critical.

Did you invest because you believe in the long-term potential of the business? Or are you only interested in making a quick profit through short-term trading? The answers to these questions can assist you in making the best decision possible. In either situation, you should act in accordance with your personal objectives. To put it another way, if you believe in the long-term potential, you should think like that. If you're looking for a speedy deal, keep that in mind.

2. Don't Give In to FOMO

We have talked repeatedly about FOMO. When hit with falling prices, it is really not the best course of action to sell your coins for those going up. This is because you do not have a guarantee that the new coin will not experience a downtrend.

3. Take Stock of the Situation

Is there any news that influences the price of Bitcoin and other cryptocurrencies? It's possible that fundamental news, rather than price action or rumor, has impacted market mood.

An objective assessment of the situation will often yield answers on the source of the market swing. For instance, China's ban on crypto platforms can lead to a market swing. Finding out this can explain the situation and guide your response.

4. It's Not Crypto If It's Not Volatile

Cryptocurrency is inherently volatile. Because there is no cash flow in crypto, traders must rely on mood changes to move the price. That implies the market can swing from frantic optimism to dismal despair in a matter of months, as happened in early 2021.

5. Consider the future

If the source of the "red" was China's ban, what are the implications for the future? Will other countries follow suit? Will the bans affect the future of crypto and its projected mass adoption? If the issue will eventually blow over, then perhaps, your investment is safe. Remember, the big bet is on the future of crypto.

6. Decide How You'll React

You'll want to think about what to do after you've cooled off and analyzed the situation and what it means for the future. Is it possible that the dangers are opportunities in disguise? If you perceive it that way, you may want to keep your position or take advantage of a price drop to invest more.

Are the dangers likely to persist, if not worsen? If this is the case, you should cut your losses and exit the game for the time being. Is the scenario a little too hazy? If you're having trouble predicting the future, consider splitting the difference and selling some of your position today while still having upside potential tomorrow. Just as we dollar-cost average into cryptocurrency, we can gradually sell small amounts to average out of our position.

7. Take a Break

Finally, do not stare at the screen all day, whatever you decide. No matter how stoic you may be, continuously watching your assets depreciate cannot be easy. So, take a break, get some air, try some other activities.

The Need for a Support Group

The community that comes with Crypto investment is one of the most exciting aspects. You may have noticed this in someone close to you; they begin crypto trading and join a group of crypto "geeks," tweeting and speaking in a certain way. While this may be off-putting or even frustrating, it is often necessary because the community serves as a source of support.

Support groups bring individuals together who are going through or have gone through similar situations. We've all heard of support groups before, especially regarding health issues. While crypto investment is not included in this category, it gives members a familiar but unique experience to bond over. People might share personal experiences and feelings, strategies, loss coping tactics, or firsthand information about trades, gains, and losses in a support group. For any potential investor interested in news, reviews, and token sales, crypto-focused social media groups and organizations can be valuable.

By joining a group, you may spend time with people who are likely to share your interest in bitcoin and communicate effectively with one another. This is especially crucial because cryptography is a new technology frontier with a lot to learn. Remember to be aware of the many scammers operating in these groups.

Other benefits include:

- Increasing your trading and investing skills.
- Obtaining a sense of control, empowerment, or hope, as well as sustaining motivation to manage your portfolio, particularly when markets are in the red.
- Obtaining relevant information on coins, tokens, and the technology that underpins them. Learning about technology, mathematics, and economics is one of the most crucial things you can do while investing in cryptocurrencies.

Support Groups are most commonly found on social media sites like Twitter, Reddit, and Discord. The majority of these groups are essentially chat rooms where anyone can post whatever they like. You can ask questions, send direct messages to the piece's author, or watch the chat for valuable information.

Other support groups may be physical meet-ups at conventions or events. Whatever is convenient for you, becoming an active community member is a crucial part of bitcoin investing.

> *"If you want to go fast, go alone; if you want to go far, go with somebody."*
>
> — AFRICAN PROVERB

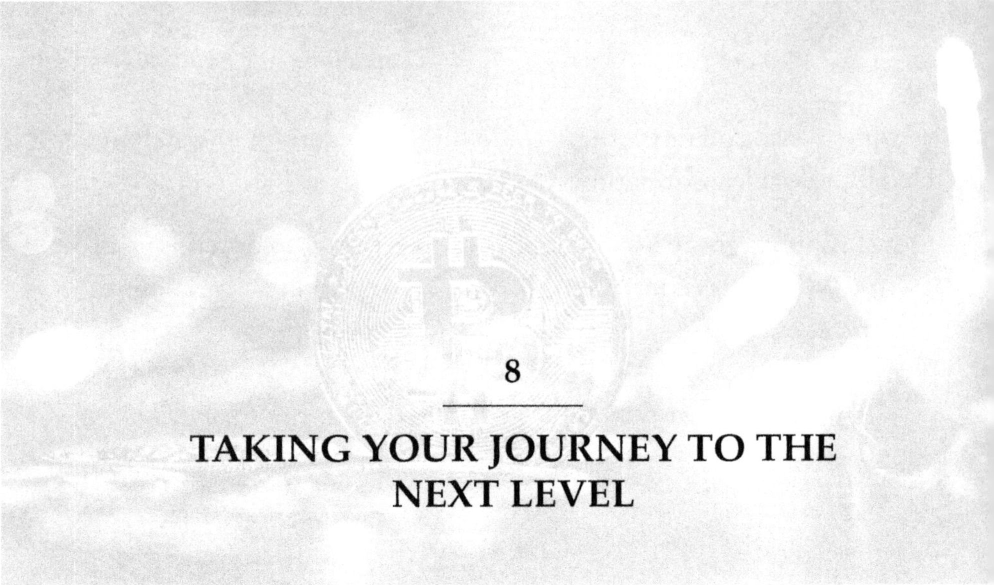

8

TAKING YOUR JOURNEY TO THE NEXT LEVEL

FOREX AND CRYPTO

The most significant distinction between crypto and Forex is what is being traded. Digital cryptocurrencies are the subject of crypto trade and investing. On the other hand, Forex deals with fiat currencies such as the US dollar and the Japanese yen.

The most significant resemblance between crypto and Forex is that they now have value concerning one another. You may look at cryptocurrencies and foreign currencies in the same way since they ebb and flow in similar ways. The primary supply and demand principle is in effect: when there are more buyers than sellers for a crypto-coin, the price of that coin rises. Like a forex bear market, a crypto bear market occurs when there are more sellers than buyers.

Both Forex and crypto respond immediately to market shocks due to efficient market absorption of news. For example, a BTC whale converting $30 million BTC to Japanese yen impacts the crypto market, just as talk of war in the White House has an impact on the value of certain US-based Forex currency pairs. Yes, you must employ several techniques and analyze various indicators to make informed decisions, but these financial instruments are not mutually exclusive.

The differences in the markets will eventually determine where you choose to put your money. Yes, you can invest in both, but the ordinary investor usually starts with one or the other. As you gain experience, you may learn about additional markets that you were unfamiliar with when you first began investing.

CRYPTO AND STOCKS

While stock trading and cryptocurrencies appear to be two different investing ideologies, traditional and contemporary, they are not as unlike as they appear. Whether dealing with stocks or crypto, the same basic trading order types are available on most retail trading platforms: market, limit, and stop (or stop-loss). To connect with financial markets nowadays, most investors log on to a digital exchange, brokerage account, mobile application, or other online platforms. With the advent of digital platforms, buying and selling stocks has never been easier. This ease has transferred to crypto, where cryptocurrency exchanges (online and on apps) have made digital asset investing as straightforward as investing in traditional markets.

The distinction between stock and cryptocurrency investing lies in the nature of what you're buying. Shares of stock traded on a stock exchange are securities representing a percentage of ownership (or equity) in the company that issued the shares. When you buy the stock, the law grants specific rights in the form of dividends, such as voting rights or a percentage of the issuer's profits.

This is not often the case with Cryptocurrencies, as they are often used differently. Many digital assets, such as ether (ETH), are utility tokens designed to be utilized in a blockchain-based ecosystem and do not reflect a legal interest in the company that issued them.

Certain types of crypto security tokens, on the other hand, are designed to function similarly to stocks—in addition to having other programmable qualities, they represent an equity stake in an issuing firm (remember our discussion on tokens in Chapter One). In some places, these tokens are guided by laws similar to those guiding shares and stocks.

The two most essential aspects of discussing and comparing stocks and cryptocurrency are risks and rewards.

The stock market is a well-established investment option with a proven track record. The stock market is notoriously volatile when it comes to risk, with stocks frequently rising and falling within the same year. On the other hand, the Stock Market has been around long enough for investors to recognize that there will almost always be a reversal. Furthermore, the stock exchange is strictly controlled. Companies must go through a rigorous process before listing their stock on the stock exchange. Companies that trade on the stock exchange are bound by rules governing transparency and the number of shares that can be issued. All of this adds up to stocks being a more secure investment option.

On the other hand, Bitcoin and cryptocurrencies have completely outperformed the stock market in terms of returns. In 2020, both Bitcoin and the stock market enjoyed remarkable success. The S&P 500 index returned 18 percent to investors, while several equities delivered life-changing returns in just a few months. The return on investment for Bitcoin in 2020 was staggering, with a 288% return.

You don't have to pick between cryptocurrency and stocks—or other sorts of assets like bonds or mutual funds—when it comes to constructing your portfolio. It's all about matching your risk tolerance and time horizon to your portfolio. Even a small investment in cryptocurrencies might make a significant difference in your portfolio if it takes off. Limiting your cryptocurrency investment also protects you from a total loss if crypto fails.

LOOKING AHEAD: WHAT DOES THE FUTURE OF MONEY LOOK LIKE?

When it comes to the future of money, there appears to be agreement that it will be digital. The key question, especially regarding cryptocurrencies, is whether the digital future of money will be dominated by cryptocurrencies like Bitcoin or the continued usage of fiat currency in digital forms, such as credit cards.

Credit card and mobile phone payments have already impacted the physical cash market. There is, however, still space for even more disruption and acceptance. According to Eswar Prasad, a senior fellow at the Brookings Institute, the actual driving factor will be central banks. As new cryptocurrencies rise and their popularity grows, central banks will respond by producing more stable forms.

Others are pessimistic. Bitcoin was intended to represent a revolution in the financial environment when it was first presented to the globe over a decade ago. But such a revolution is still a long way off. Nearly 13 years later, critics claim that the original vision has been compromised. Centralization has supplanted decentralization. Bitcoin whales, or investors with large holdings of the cryptocurrency, exert market control over its price. The democratization of mining as a means of printing money appears to have been compromised in favor of the efficiency of large-scale mining farms.

On the other hand, investors and cryptocurrency aficionados have increased their confidence in the currency's future. For crypto believers, the drawbacks are outweighed by the development of a strong and active crypto ecosystem. The cryptocurrency market is now worth $2.02 trillion, even though it did not exist a decade ago. As a result, the next ten years could be crucial for Bitcoin and cryptocurrencies in general. Nevertheless, beyond just the "financial revolutions," Bitcoin holds a lot of other prospects for investors. At the moment, cryptocurrency is torn between becoming a store of value and a transactional medium. Even though governments worldwide, such as Japan, have recognized it as a viable means of payment for goods, institutional investors are keen to join in on the action and profit from the volatility in its pricing.

However, scale and security issues have stopped both events from occurring at this time. A more secure Bitcoin ecosystem will aid widespread acceptance. Without technological advancements in its ecosystem, Bitcoin's mainstreaming as a payment mechanism (or, for that matter, its increasing attractiveness as an asset class) will be impossible. Bitcoin's blockchain must be able to process millions of transactions in a short period to be regarded as a viable investment asset or method of payment.

The crypto industry appears to be aware of this and is working on solutions. Several technologies, such as the Lightning Network, promise scalability in the company's operations. New cryptocurrencies, such as Bitcoin Cash and Bitcoin Gold, have emerged as a result of hard forks in the Bitcoin blockchain, with the goal of adjusting the ecosystem's settings to handle more transactions at a faster speed.

The ecosystem will probably gain mainstream acceptability as legislation evolves to keep up. The first ten years saw a booming market. The coming decade could usher in a slew of low-cost, high-speed payment methods that will propel cryptocurrency into the mainstream. The interest of large banks and institutions in cryptocurrencies is perhaps the most telling predictor of the currency's future. Bitcoin, according to CitiBank, might become the preferred money for international trade. This comes after both PayPal and Tesla announced cryptocurrency bets in early 2021. Tesla purchased $1.5 billion in Bitcoin, while PayPal offered to buy Curv, a crypto custodian. Bitcoin's future is still highly uncertain, according to Citi, but it is on the verge of general acceptance.

CRYPTO MINING

Bitcoin mining is the process of creating new bitcoins, and it's also how the network confirms new transactions, a vital aspect of the blockchain ledger's maintenance and development. "Mining" is carried out using high-tech hardware that solves a complex computational arithmetic problem. The first computer to complete the task receives the next block of bitcoins, and the process continues.

The goal of confirming Bitcoin transaction data is to avoid double-spending. Counterfeiting is always an issue with printed money. In most cases, though, when you spend $20 in a store, the bill is in the hands of the clerk. But it's a different scenario with digital currency. Because digital information is relatively easy to duplicate, there is a possibility that a spender may make a replica of their bitcoin and send it to a third party while keeping the original. As a result, only qualified miners are allowed to update the digital record in Bitcoin's distributed ledger. This places an additional responsibility on miners to protect the network from double-spending. In the interim, new currencies are produced to contribute to the network's security. Miners are thus motivated to safeguard the network by participating in the transaction validation process, which enhances their chances of winning newly generated coins. Transaction validation is dependent on the mining process since distributed ledgers lack a centralized authority.

A proof-of-work (PoW) consensus system has been implemented to ensure that only confirmed crypto miners can mine and validate transactions. PoW also protects the network against outside threats. Miners must deploy devices that solve complicated mathematical equations in the form of cryptographic hashes to be paid with new currency. A hash is a data chunk's shortened digital signature. Hashes are used to encrypt data sent over a public network.

Bitcoin transactions are grouped into blocks, which are then uploaded to the blockchain. Miners compete with their peers to find a hash value generated by a crypto coin transaction, and the first miner to break the code receives the reward and adds the block to the ledger. Every 210,000 blocks, the block reward is half (or roughly every four years). It was 50 in 2009. In 2013, the incentive was reduced to $25, and in 2016, it was reduced to $12.5. The reward was reduced to 6.25 at Bitcoin's most recent halving event.

Using a hash function, each block refers to the one before it, creating an unbroken chain of blocks that all lead back to the original. As a result, network peers may verify if certain blocks are valid and whether the miners that confirmed each block solved the hash correctly to collect the reward.

Transaction fees are another motivation for bitcoin miners to participate in the process. Miners receive fees from any transactions in that block of transactions in addition to prizes. Miners are paid fees for processing transactions that network users will pay as Bitcoin reaches its scheduled limit of 21 million (estimated around 2140). These fees ensure that miners continue to be motivated to mine and maintain the network. The assumption is that after the halving events are completed, there will be enough competition for these fees to keep them low.

Bitcoin mining is based on a math puzzle miners must solve to get bitcoin rewards. Proof of work (PoW) is a problem that refers to the computational work that miners put into mining bitcoin. The mining puzzle can be described as guesswork. In Bitcoin's PoW algorithm, miners attempt to generate a 64-digit hexadecimal number called a hash that is less than or equal to a target hash.

Here's an illustration of how the procedure works. Let's say I ask my friends to guess a number between 100 and 1000 that I've come up with and written down on a piece of paper. My friends don't have to predict the precise number; all they have to accomplish is be the first to guess a figure that is less than or equal to mine. If I'm thinking of the number 350 and a friend says 400, they lose because 400 is higher than 350. However, if one friend guesses 300 and another gets 320, the latter wins because 320 is closer to 350 than 300. The Bitcoin mining math challenge is essentially the same as the situation described above, but with 64-digit hexadecimal values and hundreds of processing devices.

Strategies for Cutting Down Losses

Stick to Your Trading Strategy

Your trading plan is the result of extensive research. It is precisely to cut losses that you require a trading plan. You may feel compelled to close or open a specific order from time to time. The market is going great, and you are lucky. However, keep in mind that trades that aren't in your plan aren't there for a reason. This is your non-anxious self telling you to take a breath and control your risks before you go insane.

Make Use of Stop-Loss Orders

When the currency hits a specific level, this function allows you to exit a losing trade. Most cryptocurrency trading platforms have this feature. For example, if you have a maximum of $50 to trade on one Binance Coin (BNB), which is currently worth $580. That means your stop-loss should be set at $480. The order will be automatically closed if the coin falls below this level, limiting your losses.

Waiting It Out: HODLing

While the adage "it's not a loss until it's sold" is only partially true, it has some merit. Unrealized losses occur when the worth of your assets has decreased after you purchased them, and they are only realized when they are sold for less than the original purchase price.

Over the long term, Bitcoin has continuously trended upward. Even if prices are decreasing due to a momentary market correction or a lengthier bear market, history teaches that prices will eventually recover due to economic causes like scarcity.

Take Profit

Converting some of your volatile crypto holdings for more stable assets is one of the safest ways to minimize crypto volatility and protect yourself during a market downturn. In a cryptocurrency bull market, this can assist an investor to 'lock-in' their balance, reducing risk and the need to manage their portfolio and stress levels actively.

Stablecoins like USDT try to keep their value constant. Changing a portion of your portfolio to stable-value assets reduces your exposure to price fluctuations when the markets are quiet.

CRYPTO DECODED

Like every industry or trade, cryptocurrency comes with its set of terms and jargon. These can often be off-putting for beginners while having the simplest meanings. We have made a list of some of the most common terms with concise explanations.

Altcoin

The term "altcoin" is a combination of the words "alternative" and "coin," and it refers to any digital money that isn't Bitcoin.

Bitcoin

This is the first and most popular cryptocurrency. In 2008, the mysterious "Satoshi Nakamoto" Bitcoin. Despite the rise of many altcoins, the currency continues to dominate the news.

Bitcoin Cash

Bitcoin underwent its first "fork" (see below) in August 2017, splitting into bitcoin and bitcoin cash, which are now two completely different currencies.

Block

A block is a collection of transaction data that is permanently stored. After it's finished, it's stored in a blockchain (the ledger), which works as a permanent record of all previous data blocks. After that, a new block is created for new data to be stored. Each block also includes a mathematical riddle with a unique solution, and additional blocks cannot be added to the blockchain until the answer is provided.

Confirmation

Every 10 minutes, a new block is added to the blockchain through mining. This block confirms any new transactions, known as the confirmation process. Depending on the size of the transaction, certain sellers may demand several confirmations from various blocks.

Fiat

This refers to money issued by the government. Fiat currency, such as the US dollar or the British pound, is legal tender whose value is guaranteed by the government that issued it.

Fork

A fork establishes two separate versions of the blockchain, which run parallel on different parts of the network. A "hard fork" makes previously invalid transactions valid and vice versa, whereas a "soft fork" makes previously valid transactions invalid but not the other way around.

FUD

Fear, uncertainty, and doubt are abbreviated as FUD. Often used in bitcoin forums as a slam against skeptics who are "promoting FUD again."

Futures

Futures trading is a way to speculate on the value of assets, such as cryptocurrency, without really owning them. Cryptocurrency futures, like commodity or stock futures, allow traders to speculate on the price of a digital currency in the future.

Hashing

The process of mining bitcoin or another cryptocurrency by employing cryptographic hash functions to solve a mathematical problem within it.

HODL

This simply means "Hold." It was created as slang when someone entered HODL instead of HOLD on a bitcoin forum. It has become the war cry of dedicated cryptocurrency investors who believe their investment will pay off one day.

ICO

Initial Coin Offering (ICO) is a popular and often unregulated means to generate funds for new cryptocurrency enterprises. In exchange for more established cryptocurrencies, a portion of the new currency is sold to backers as blockchain "tokens."

Limit Order

A limit order is used to buy or sell a specific item at a pre-determined price, even better if feasible. A buy limit order can be filled at or below the limit price, whereas a sell limit order can be filled at or above the limit price.

Market Order

A market order is an order to purchase or sell an asset as soon as feasible at (or near) the current bid (for a sale order) or ask (for a buy order). A market order ensures that the order will be fulfilled, but it does not guarantee that the price will be met.

Meme Coin

A meme coin is a cryptocurrency inspired by or created as a joke in the same manner that a meme is. A unit of such a cryptocurrency is referred to as a meme coin. Dogecoin, a cryptocurrency based on the Doge meme, is perhaps the most well-known cryptocurrency, usually referred to as a meme coin.

Mining

The process of discovering new bitcoins, which entails assembling recent transactions into blocks and using hashing to attempt to solve a computationally tough puzzle.

Mining Rig

A computer that has been specifically developed to mine cryptocurrencies.

Node

A node is a computer that is connected to the bitcoin network. These nodes validate and transmit transactions while obtaining a copy of the entire blockchain.

Private Key vs. Public Key

A cryptographic code that enables a user to receive cryptocurrency into their account. The public key is made publicly available through a publicly accessible directory, while the private key is kept private by its owner. Because the key pair is mathematically linked, whatever is encrypted with a public key can only be decoded with the private key that corresponds to it.

Sats

A "satoshi" or "sat" is the lowest fraction of a bitcoin. It is named after Satoshi Nakamoto and symbolizes one-hundred-millionths of a bitcoin.

Shitcoin

A cryptocurrency with little to no value or a digital currency with no immediate, visible use is referred to as a shitcoin. The term is sometimes used as a derogatory term to characterize altcoins or cryptocurrencies that emerged after bitcoin became prominent.

Stablecoins

A "stablecoin" is a cryptocurrency whose value is tied to another asset class, such as a fiat currency or gold, to keep its value stable. Because their prices are fixed to a reserve asset like the US dollar or gold, stablecoins link cryptocurrency and daily fiat currency. Volatility is greatly reduced as a result of this.

Stop/Stop Loss

A stop (or stop-loss) order is used to prevent excessive losses. When the price of a security reaches a specified level, termed the stop price, an order to close the position is made. When the stop price is reached, the stop order becomes a market order.

Technical Analysis

Technical analysis is the process of obtaining data from cryptocurrency markets and analyzing it statistically to forecast future price movements. This may appear to be both technical and complex but simply put, the trader uses the chart's historical price data to predict where the price will go in the future.

Token

Funders are given tokens of the new cryptocurrency in exchange for their liquid cash or liquid cryptocurrency when a new cryptocurrency is created through an ICO (see above). If and when the new currency targets are met and it launches, these tokens are meant to become currency units.

Whale

Cryptocurrency traders and speculators use this word to characterize players who own large quantities of bitcoin. As their name implies, whales are the largest swimmers in the cryptocurrency pond.

As a result, Satoshi Nakamoto is the largest whale of them all. When these whales buy or sell, they can enormously impact markets. Therefore, other traders keep an eye out for signals of their moves.

FINAL WORDS

Twenty-five years ago, tech experts and other people in the tech industry prophesied that the internet was the future of technology. While on the other hand, many people in traditional institutions said the internet was no more than a passing phase. Less than three decades later, the internet has revolutionized the world, and most people who made early investments in the future of the internet are better for it. Most crypto experts say investing in cryptocurrency now is like in the early days of the internet.

One of the fascinating features of cryptocurrencies is that they solve various issues arising from conventional currencies. The blockchain technology upon which cryptocurrencies are based is secure and incredibly reliable. If much of the current internet assets are centralized in the hands of a few big technology companies, decentralized projects, like Bitcoin, can democratize and distribute not just money but also computing, smart contracts, and many other applications. Experts agree that it has great potential to improve many sectors of our daily lives.

The key takeaway is this—while cryptocurrency investing is risky, it may hold the promise of life-changing returns, especially for people with a long-term view. The best way to get started is first to understand cryptocurrencies and not jump in headfirst. And that is what this book has done. Together, we have begun our journey into crypto investing. We discussed the three things necessary for understanding cryptocurrencies—the cryptocurrency itself, the underlying technology, and the practical steps of investing.

We have talked about cryptocurrencies, what they are, and why they are unique. We looked at the types, where to buy and sell them. We provided a Step-By-Step Guide on How to Buy Cryptocurrency on Binance. A summary of all things crypto was provided in our 12 Things to Know Before Crypto Investing.

To better understand cryptocurrencies, we delved into Blockchain, which is the technology behind them. We dug into mining, how coins are created, and how to store your crypto in wallets.

Then, we discussed other related issues such as risk management, crypto taxes, and protecting yourselves from crypto scams. Lastly, we featured the Jargon Buster, where we have a glossary of crypto terms and provide concise explanations for each term.

From investing to tech to taxes, we have covered the bases for you. The purpose of this book is to make you as informed as possible about this potentially world-changing technology. We hope what we've discussed in this book gives you the information you need to make wise crypto investment decisions.

However, all the knowledge in this book will amount to nothing if you don't take action toward starting your cryptocurrency investment journey. Take your time, do your own research, and never stop learning. We wish you the very best of luck in your investing journey to financial freedom and beyond.

We hope you have found this book useful and enjoyable. If so, it would mean the world to us if you could take a minute to leave a review.

COULD WE ASK A FAVOR?

Thank you so much for purchasing our book and for making it all the way to the end. We work hard to make our books the highest quality possible.

Could we ask a favor?

Could you please consider posting a review?

Reviews are the best way to support the work of independent authors like us. Your feedback helps us write better books that educate and empower you to make money and create financial freedom.

Leaving a review only takes 2 minutes and would mean the world to us.

REFERENCES

Ballentine, C., Kantor, A., & Schmidt, B. (2021, September 25). The Fight to Control the $2 Trillion Crypto Market Is Heating Up. Www.bloomberg.com. https://www.bloomberg.com/news/articles/2021-09-25/who-will-control-crypto-and-bitcoin-btc-us-china-fight-rattles-investors

Can The Government Regulate Cryptocurrency? (2021, January 12). The NYU Dispatch. https://wp.nyu.edu/dispatch/can-the-government-regulate-cryptocurrency/

Davies. (n.d.). 4 things that make society doubt about cryptocurrency effectiveness. Daviescoin.io. https://daviescoin.io/blog/4-things-that-make-society-doubt-about-cryptocurrency-effectiveness

Kenton, W. (2019). Bitcoin Mining, Explained. Investopedia. https://www.investopedia.com/terms/b/bitcoin-mining.asp

Here's How You Convert Your Cryptocurrency Into Cash. (2021, August 16). Retrieved December 3, 2021, from NDTV Gadgets 360 website: https://gadgets.ndtv.com/cryptocurrency/features/convert-cryptocurrency-into-cash-explained-how-to-2511389

Miller, R. (2021, March 23). Bitcoin Is A Cryptocurrency, But Is It Money? Retrieved December 3, 2021, from Forbes website: https://www.forbes.com/sites/rmiller/2021/03/23/bitcoin-is-a-cryptocurrency-but-is-it-money/amp/

The Future of Money: Is Bitcoin Money? (2021, August 5). Retrieved December 3, 2021, from Alec Torelli's Official Website website: https://www.alectorelli.com/is-bitcoin-money/

The Future of Money: Is Bitcoin Money? (2021, August 5). Retrieved December 3, 2021, from Alec Torelli's Official Website website: https://www.alectorelli.com/is-bitcoin-money/

Kelleher, J. (2019). Why do Bitcoins have value? Retrieved December 3, 2021, from Investopedia website: https://www.investopedia.com/ask/answers/100314/why-do-bitcoins-have-value.asp

Hayes. (2019). What Happens to Bitcoin after All 21 Million Are Mined? Retrieved December 4, 2021, from Investopedia website: https://www.investopedia.com/tech/what-happens-bitcoin-after-21-million-mined/

Types and Categories of Cryptocurrency | executium Trading System. (2020, May 21). Retrieved December 4, 2021, from executium.com website: https://executium.com/crypto-categories/342613-types-and-categories-of-cryptocurrency/

M. Laura. (2021, November 22). Various Types of Cryptocurrency: How Many Cryptocurrencies are There? Retrieved December 5, 2021, from BitDegree.org Crypto Exchanges website: https://www.bitdegree.org/crypto/tutorials/types-of-cryptocurrency

Rossolillo, N. (2018, April 5). Types of Cryptocurrency. Retrieved November 29, 2021, from The Motley Fool website: https://www.fool.com/investing/stock-market/market-sectors/financials/cryptocurrency-stocks/types-of-cryptocurrencies/

What Causes Cryptocurrency Price Fluctuations? (Explained) . (2021, April 2). Retrieved November 30, 2021, from www.coinario.com website: https://www.coinario.com/info/what-causes-cryptocurrency-price-fluctuations

https://studentedge.org/article/why-does-the-price-of-cryptocurrency-fluctuate-so-much. (2018, December 17). Retrieved November 31, 2021, from Student Edge website: https://studentedge.org/article/why-does-the-price-of-cryptocurrency-fluctuate-so-much

Investdiva. (2018, July 20). 7 Risks of Cryptocurrency Investing and How to Handle Them. Invest Diva. https://investdiva.com/investing-guide/risks-of-cryptocurrency-investing/

Frankenfield, J. (2021, November 30). *What Is a Crypto Token?* Investopedia.

accessed on 11/23/2021 https://www.investopedia.com/terms/c/crypto-token.asp

Times of India(2021, November 2). "Tokens: How are cryptocurrencies and tokens different?" accessed on 11/23/2021

https://timesofindia.indiatimes.com/business/cryptocurrency/blockchain/how-are-cryptocurrencies-and-tokens-different/articleshow/87483152.cms

(2016, November 18). *Blockchain - Benefits, Drawbacks and Everything You Need to Know*. https://marutitech.com/benefits-of-blockchain/#How_does_blockchain_work

Raghav Chopra. (2017, December 2). Explaining Blockchain as if you are a 5 year old Kid. Medium; accessed on 11/24/2021

https://medium.com/@chopra.raghav2180/explaining-blockchain-as-if-you-are-a-5-year-old-kid-df543f137f81

Coinpedia. (2021, January 20). Benefits and Challenges in Investing New Cryptocurrencies. Coinpedia - Fintech & Cryptocurreny News Media| Crypto Guide. https://coinpedia.org/guest-post/benefits-and-challenges-investing-new-cryptocurrencies/

Bass, M. (2021, September 30). Why You Always Need a Plan or an Exit Strategy When Trading Crypto? ICharts. Accessed on 11/29/2021 https://www.icharts.net/always-need-plan-or-exit-strategy-when-trading/

Bitvo. (2020, November 10). Manage your crypto trading risks with a plan. Bitvo. https://bitvo.com/crypto-trading-risk-management/

Reutzel, B. (2021, October 11). How to invest in cryptocurrency: Exchanges, apps, wallets and more. CNBC. https://www.cnbc.com/amp/select/how-to-invest-in-cryptocurrency-exchanges-apps-wallets-and-more/

Shashank. (2021, January 12). Top 10 reasons to learn Blockchain | Why Blockchain. Edureka. https://www.edureka.co/blog/top-10-reasons-to-learn-blockchain/amp/

Pratt, M. (2021, June 2). Top 10 Benefits of Blockchain Technology for Business. SearchCIO. https://searchcio.techtarget.com/feature/Top-10-benefits-of-blockchain-technology-for-business?amp=1

Brockman, K. (2021, August 15). 3 Reasons I'm Investing in Cryptocurrency. The Motley Fool. https://www.fool.com/investing/2021/08/15/3-reasons-im-investing-in-cryptocurrency/

The Times. (2021, December 13). Should I Invest In Bitcoin? Www.-thetimes.co.uk. https://www.thetimes.co.uk/money-mentor/article/invest-bitcoin-cryptocurrencies/

Mix, P. (2021, August 5). 5 reasons why you should invest in cryptocurrency. Pulse Nigeria. https://www.pulse.ng/business/5-reasons-why-you-should-invest-in-cryptocurrency/gmvc7zy.amp

The Top 15 Reasons to Invest in Cryptocurrencies | Trading Education. (2021, July 23). Trading-Education.com. https://trading-education.com/top-15-reasons-to-invest-in-cryptocurrencies

Reiff, N. (2021, August 24). Question: Why Should Anyone Invest in Crypto? Investopedia. https://www.investopedia.com/tech/question-why-should-anyone-invest-crypto

Yahoo Finance. (2021, November 17). How to introduce smart security strategies to protect your investment. Finance.yahoo.com. https://finance.yahoo.com/news/investing-in-crypto-heres-how-to-begin-172724140-145227544.html

Tretina, K. (2021, July 12). How To Buy Cryptocurrency. Forbes Advisor. https://www.forbes.com/advisor/investing/how-to-buy-cryptocurrency/

Esajian, P. (2021, October 26). How To Invest In Cryptocurrency: A Beginner's Guide. FortuneBuilders. https://www.fortunebuilders.com/how-to-invest-in-cryptocurrency/

FXSTREET. (n.d.). How to Choose a Cryptocurrency Broker. Brokers that offer cryptos. FXStreet. Retrieved December 14, 2021, from https://www.fxstreet.com/cryptocurrencies/resources/brokers-cryptocurrency-broker

Axim Dialy. (2021, November 4). How to Choose the Best Broker for Cryptocurrency Trading? Axim Daily. https://www.aximdaily.com/2021/11/11/best-broker-cryptocurrency-trading/#What_is_a_Cryptocurrency_Broker

Murdock, M. (2012, August 11). How to choose a cryptocurrency (and crypto platform). Morning Brew. https://www.morningbrew.com/daily/stories/2021/08/11/choose-cryptocurrency-crypto-platform

King Passive. (2018, February 17). 10 Easy Ways To Decide Which Cryptocurrency To Invest In! Kingpassive.com. https://kingpassive.com/which-cryptocurrency-to-invest-in/

Brockman, K. (2021a, June 24). Cryptocurrency: When Is the Right Time to Buy? The Motley Fool. https://www.fool.com/investing/2021/06/24/when-is-the-right-time-to-buy-cryptocurrency/

Van Der Wielen, Z. (2021, April 30). Crypto exit strategy – When to sell your coins. AnycoinDirect. https://anycoindirect.eu/en/blog/crypto-exit-strategy-when-to-sell-your-coins

Hayes, A. (2021, December 4). How to Buy Bitcoin. Investopedia. https://www.investopedia.com/articles/investing/082914/basics-buying-and-investing-bitcoin.asp#how-to-sell-bitcoin

Conway, L. (2021, February 28). What are the Safest Ways to Store Bitcoin? Investopedia. https://www.investopedia.com/news/bitcoin-safe-storage-cold-wallet/

Rudri Srinivas. (2020, August 17). How to Safeguard Your Cryptocurrency Wallet from Digital Exploits. CISO MAG | Cyber Security Magazine. https://cisomag.eccouncil.org/cryptocurrency-wallet-security/amp/

Blufish. (2021, June 25). The different types of crypto wallets, explained. AZ Big Media. https://azbigmedia.com/business/the-different-types-of-crypto-wallets-explained/

Mitra, M. (2021, August 11). Diversification Is the Key to Investing in Stocks and Bonds. Here's Why It Can Work for Crypto, Too. Money. https://money.com/diversification-crypto-benefits-limits/?amp=true

Ranjan, A. (2021, September 1). Why you should diversify investments in Cryptocurrencies | Personal-finance News – India TV. Www.indiatvnews.com. https://www.indiatvnews.com/amp/

business/personal-finance-why-you-should-diversify-investments-in-cryptocurrencies-730750

Mohit. (2020, December 15). Bitcoin vs. Traditional Assets: Who is Ahead Right Now? Mohit Tater. https://mohittater.com/bitcoin-vs-traditional-assets/

Royal, J., & Voight, K. (2021, December 10). What Is Cryptocurrency? Beginners Guide to Digital Cash. NerdWallet. https://www.nerdwallet.com/article/investing/cryptocurrency-7-things-to-know

Ross, J. (2021, June 10). The Biggest Companies in the World in 2021. Visual Capitalist. https://www.visualcapitalist.com/the-biggest-companies-in-the-world-in-2021/

From avoiding FOMO to having a plan, 5 key ways to manage a crypto down cycle. (n.d.). Www.coinbase.com. Retrieved December 22, 2021, from https://www.coinbase.com/learn/tips-and-tutorials/how-to-minimize-your-losses-during-a-falling-market

Hayes, A. (2019). Stablecoin. Investopedia. https://www.investopedia.com/terms/s/stablecoin.asp

Which Is The Best Cryptocurrency For Long-Term Investment? Find Out. (2021, September 20). NDTV.com. https://www.ndtv.com/business/these-cryptocurrencies-are-best-for-long-term-investment-2531674/amp/1

Adams, R. (2021, May 21). 9 Ways to Cut Crypto Taxes Down to the Bone. Kiplinger. https://www.kiplinger.com/taxes/capital-gains-tax/602825/ways-to-cut-crypto-taxes-down-to-the-bone?amp

Hong, E. (2021, January 7). How Does Bitcoin Mining Work? Investopedia. https://www.investopedia.com/tech/how-does-bitcoin-mining-work/

Tepper, T. (2021, August 1). Best Crypto Exchanges Of 2021. Forbes Advisor. https://www.forbes.com/advisor/investing/best-crypto-exchanges/

Mehra, D. (2021, November 21). What are the risks of investing in cryptocurrencies? Khaleej Times. https://www.khaleejtimes.com/cryptocurrency/what-are-the-risks-of-investing-in-cryptocurrencies

Cryptocurrency investment: Worried about risk in cryptocurrency? Here's how to invest without buying any token - The Economic Times. (2021, October 7). M.economictimes.com. https://m.economictimes.com/markets/cryptocurrency/worried-about-risk-in-cryptocurrency-heres-how-to-invest-without-buying-any-token/amp_articleshow/86829852.cms

Montag, A. (2018, August 9). Yale economist: Here's how likely it is that bitcoin will become worthless. CNBC. https://www.cnbc.com/amp/2018/08/09/yale-economist-how-likely-it-is-that-bitcoin-will-become-worthless.html

Crypto Risk Management. (2021, April 23). Gemini. https://www.gemini.com/cryptopedia/crypto-risk-management-what-does-it-mean

Avoiding cryptocurrency scams | Coinbase Help. (n.d.). Help.coinbase.com. https://help.coinbase.com/en/coinbase/privacy-and-security/avoiding-phishing-and-scams/avoiding-cryptocurrency-scams

Voight, K., & Rosen, A. (2021, September 24). What to Do When Crypto Is Crashing. NerdWallet. https://www.nerdwallet.com/article/investing/crypto-crash

Royal, J. (2021, September 16). Bitcoin And Crypto Prices Are Volatile — What To Do When They're Crashing | Bankrate.

Www.bankrate.com. https://www.bankrate.com/investing/bitcoin-and-crypto-crash-what-investors-should-do/amp/

Frankenfield, J. (2021, June 24). What Is Shitcoin? Investopedia. https://www.investopedia.com/terms/s/shitcoin.asp

Bitcoinist. (2021, June). List of Top 10 Crypto Telegram Channels and Groups | Bitcoinist.com. Bitcoinist. https://bitcoinist.com/list-of-top-10-crypto-telegram-channels-and-groups/

Mayo Clinic. (2018). How to choose the right support group. Mayo Clinic. https://www.mayoclinic.org/healthy-lifestyle/stress-management/in-depth/support-groups/art-20044655

Bigmore, R. (2018, May 18). Time to bust the cryptocurrency jargon. The Telegraph. https://www.telegraph.co.uk/technology/digital-money/how-to-understand-cryptocurrency-terminology/

Morris, J. (2021, May 22). Short-Term vs. Long-Term Investment in Cryptocurrency: Build Your Investment Strategy. LetsExchange Blog. https://letsexchange.io/blog/short-term-vs-long-term-investment-in-cryptocurrency-build-your-investment-strategy/amp/

Reinicke, C. (2021, July 27). Cryptocurrencies can be a tool for building personal wealth long-term. CNBC. https://www.cnbc.com/2021/07/27/cryptocurrencies-can-be-a-tool-for-building-personal-wealth-long-term.html

Sharma, R. (2021, August 25). What Will Happen To Bitcoin In The Next Decade? Investopedia. https://www.investopedia.com/tech/what-will-happen-bitcoin-next-decade/

The future of money: The end of cash and the rise of digital currencies. (2021, August 26). Brookings. https://www.brookings.edu/events/the-future-of-money-the-end-of-cash-and-the-rise-of-digital-currencies/amp/

Evans, Brian (2018, December 27). "The 3 Lessons Missing Out on Bitcoin Taught Me About Trusting Myself. Crunchbase".

Accessed on 11/19/2021

https://about.crunchbase.com/blog/missing-out-bitcoin/

Reese, Riley (2017) "Cryptocurrencies to Consider Buying Over Bitcoin If You Missed Out"

Accessed on 11/19/2021 https://vocal.media/theChain/cryptocurrencies-to-consider-buying-over-bitcoin-if-you-missed-out

Conroy, Cato (2017) "How to Deal with Cryptocurrency FOMO"

Accessed on 11/19/2021

https://vocal.media/theChain/cryptocurrencies-to-consider-buying-over-bitcoin-if-you-missed-out

Subburaj, Vikram (2021, October 3) "When is it a good time to invest in Bitcoin, explained" The News Minute https://www.thenewsminute.com/article/when-it-good-time-invest-bitcoin-explained-156043

Carmody, B. (2018, January 5). Bitcoin IRAs: Evaluating the Risk vs. Reward. Inc.com. Accessed on 11/29/2021 https://www.inc.com/bill-carmody/bitcoin-iras-evaluating-risk-vs-reward.html

Jouman Hajjar, A. (2021, May 9). *Cryptocurrency ETFs: Pros, Cons & Alternatives*. Research.aimultiple.com. https://research.aimultiple.com/crypto-etfs/

Young, M. (2021, October 25). *The Pros and Cons of Bitcoin ETF.* Altcoin Buzz. https://www.altcoinbuzz.io/cryptocurrency-news/the-pros-and-cons-of-bitcoin-etf/

Binance.com (2021, July 30) How to Buy Cryptocurrency on Binance Homepage

https://www.binance.com/en/support/faq/400c38f5e0cd4b46a1d0805c296b5582

Printed in Great Britain
by Amazon

16821784R00088